Running Your Own
RESTAURANT

Running Your Own
RESTAURANT

Diane Hughes
and
Godfrey Golzen

THE
KOGAN PAGE
Working for Yourself
SERIES

Dedication

For my parents
Thelma and Costas Stefani
with love and thanks

Diane Hughes
August 1985

First published in Great Britain in 1986
by Kogan Page Limited
120 Pentonville Road
London N1 9JN

Reprinted 1987

British Library Cataloguing in Publication Data

Hughes, Diane
    Running your own restaurant.—(Kogan Page
    working for yourself series)
    1. Restaurant management—Great Britain
    I. Title   II. Golzen, Godfrey
    647′.95′068   TX911.3.M27

    ISBN 0-85038-850-3 Hbk
    ISBN 0-85038-851-1

Typeset by Mathematical Composition Setters Ltd,
Salisbury, Wiltshire
Printed and bound in Great Britain by
Biddles Ltd, Guildford and King's Lynn

Contents

Chapter 1

Introduction

Many facts of life today make restaurants a booming business. More working wives, more leisure time, extra disposable income for many people and a growing sophistication in eating habits all point to a healthy future for restaurants as part of the growing 'leisure and services' industry.

It isn't easy . . .

But running a restaurant isn't easy. Apart from the sheer hard physical work, catering can be surprisingly lonely, socially crippling, and financially disastrous. Restaurants always figure high in the bankruptcy league along with builders and retailers. Over 10,000 caterers a year disappear — many of them down Carey Street with a call into the divorce courts on the way. Advance warning could have helped.

So if you imagine that running your own restaurant is little more than an extension of cooking for the family or a pleasant and profitable way of entertaining friends, this book should dispel some of those fantasies and help you work towards success.

. . . but it can be fun

Once you are prepared for the hard work, long hours, and the struggle to make a profit initially, running a restaurant can be great fun and very fulfilling. It can provide a superb way of life, often in an attractive part of the country you might not otherwise be free to choose.

If you do strike the right combination of factors which make a successful restaurant you could become well off, a fashion leader or a pillar of the community, depending on your style.

To succeed, you need to be totally committed to your restaurant. You also need a basic flair for the business and some relevant experience or ability. The most important points are outlined in the following pages.

Personality

More than anything, you must like people and care about their well-being. Providing food and hospitality is a sociable business and a responsible one. People are putting their welfare in your hands so you need a practical, well-organised approach with an aptitude for detail as well as flair with food.

Sociability is important — both customers and staff want a pleasant person to deal with — but this need not entail becoming bosom friends with each customer. Indeed, an overwhelming welcome could put some people off. But meeting your clients should be one of the pleasures of restaurant work and not a nuisance, as some places seem to find it.

You should be in good health to cope with the physical demands of the work, with a temperament which can take in its stride the different pressures of busy and slack times.

Knowledge and experience

Most people who start out to run their own restaurant begin on a relatively small scale so it is likely that you will need to handle all aspects of the business yourself — a jack of all trades, in fact. These areas fall into four broad categories:

- Food and cooking
- Business management
- Managing people
- Sales and marketing.

Food and cooking
An interest in food is an obvious point but one that some people still overlook. Professional catering, however, calls for a more organised and proficient interest than family feeding: efficient buying to find the right quality and price; correct preparation to produce a consistent dish in the right quantity with minimum waste, all to strict deadlines; a full understanding of food hygiene and safety measures to ensure that food is fit to eat. All of this calls for experience and skills which you may need to build before you open for business.

Business management
You should already have or plan to gain enough knowledge to keep a tight rein on your expenses and a tight control on your cash. You should know what each meal costs and how to price it

so that you make the profit margins you need. You will have to account for your takings to the VAT man and others, so a sound and simple accounting system should be within your scope. This is not difficult but it can be tedious if you hate figure work.

If you can produce a simple budget and cash flow projection it will help you to make money available for overhead expenses even when business is slack and income is in a trough.

Managing people

Whether you are working with your spouse, in partnership with a friend or using paid staff, you will need to work closely together as a team, often under pressure and when you are all tired.

Whether you are the proprietor, director or manager, the team spirit which develops will depend on your managerial skills. Such skills often come down to common sense and sensitivity but, if you know that communicating with people is not your strong point, there are some excellent books on the importance of defining responsibilities clearly, motivation and management style.

Good management of the people working for you will have a great influence on the service your customers receive so some preparation is valuable.

Sales and marketing

Some flair for sales and promotion will be a help. Although you can build a sound reputation for good food, good value and the right atmosphere, the word will spread more quickly if you can use the power of publicity. On a day-to-day level, the design of your restaurant will contribute to the 'ambience' or atmosphere which is an important part of the 'eating out experience' which people buy.

Similarly, the design of signs, menus and the occasional advertisement or promotional item all convey an image which you can control if you are aware of it.

Working for yourself

The responsibility and the rewards are far greater when you work for yourself. You have more control over the way you work and the direction of your business. It is your money and your livelihood at stake and yours will be the ultimate gain or loss.

In theory, at least, you have the freedom to choose your own hours of work, your holidays and your work colleagues. In fact, especially in catering, the business will probably decide these things for you, leaving you perhaps less freedom than an employee. Staff are not always easy to find and during illness you will have to cope.

Working for yourself can be lonely. You have to take decisions which could make or break the business and when a problem occurs you may not have anyone to discuss it with.

If you have staff you will be 'the boss', however well you get on together, and that means there will be a distance between 'you' and 'them'.

Getting to know other caterers in the area is a good idea; it may not be easy but still, take the initiative and introduce yourself and you may find you have an ally.

In short, working for yourself will be more demanding and more stimulating than being an employee and if you are successful, the rewards — material and otherwise — will be far greater.

Will you succeed?

Even the most experienced, highly trained restaurateurs make mistakes and open restaurants which fail for a whole variety of reasons. Others succeed for indefinable reasons, against all the odds.

However, there are fundamental mistakes which are common to most failed restaurants. These include a lack of understanding by the owner about what is involved, a blinkered view of what makes people eat out and what they expect when they do, the wrong location and bad business management.

The best way to increase your chances of success is to read as much as you can about the business in magazines, newspapers, trade periodicals and books. Then, get some practical experience if you have none. Working in a restaurant is quite different from knowing it as a customer. Try to work somewhere which is similar to the restaurant you want to open and, if necessary, advertise until you find the opportunity you need.

Many local colleges offer courses in catering and related business subjects which are another useful source of experience.

Finally, you should be in a position to prepare a detailed plan for your restaurant. This should cover as much detail as possible — from the amount of space you need to the price you must charge for each dish; from the total overheads you expect to pay to the staff you will need and the hours they will be on duty.

Planning in this detail will help you to identify the problems before they arise. It will also fuel your enthusiasm and contribute to your ultimate success. And there is no reason why you should not succeed as a newcomer. Indeed, the flair and enthusiasm and the fresh approach of newcomers is the lifeblood of the restaurant business. Chain restaurants run by large companies are designed for mass appeal and often lack the personal touch and imaginative style of private, individually run restaurants. These remain the best in the business — at all levels — so think hard, prepare for reality rather than fantasy, and good luck!

Chapter 2

Starting a Business

Location

The American hotel magnate Conrad Hilton, when asked what the three most important factors in making a hotel successful were, replied, 'Location, location and location'. The same principle applies to restaurants, but the way it works in the socially and economically complex environment of the modern consumer society is not as simple as it was when restaurants in the main simply served the needs of travellers and, later on, shoppers. Now that eating has become part of the leisure industry, getting the location right has become much more difficult than simply finding sites close to stations or on busy high streets.

That point is illustrated by two restaurants located close to the place where this chapter is being written. They face each other on opposite sides of a south London suburban street. One restaurant has aimed at a quality clientele and shows a menu in its window on which few items are priced at under £3. It is open only in the evenings and is always full. The much cheaper one on the opposite corner is a wine bar at lunch-time and a restaurant in the evenings. It changes hands every six months and has been a consistent failure with every owner. The problem is that it relies on passing trade of which there is not much on an ordinary suburban street. The other restaurant has established a reputation for gourmet food and it has been mentioned by several food writers, and customers come from quite a wide area to seek it out. Location, in other words, is not simply a question of sheer geography or even of the economic prosperity of a neighbourhood; it is a matter of the appropriateness of the type of trade the owner is trying to attract.

Types of restaurant

Eating places come in many varieties largely because there is an infinitely wider choice of food available even in ordinary supermarkets than there was 20 years ago. The demand has been generated by the fact that people travel more and have also become more adventurous about what they eat. But despite the wide diversity of restaurants and types of cuisine, at any rate in cities, they do fall into definable categories. These determine the way each place functions.

- *Fast food* restaurants need high visibility, simple decor usually in primary colours, inexpensive but sturdy furniture which can be easily cleaned, and bright lighting. The food is of the type that can be prepared in a production line and appeals to a broad, but from the eating point of view, fairly unsophisticated public. Because of the importance of visibility and location on key sites — motorway restaurants are the ultimate example of fast food — rentals are likely to be high.

- *Snack bars*. Whereas both the decor and the meals in fast food outlets tend to be aimed at the younger end of the market, snack bars appeal to an older segment of it though they also offer cheap, quick meals. They are much smaller in area than fast food restaurants and prime locations are less important — in fact they are even to be found down side streets running off main ones. The clientele for snack bars, being older and less affluent than that for fast food outlets, is more price conscious.

- *Ethnic*. Chinese, Indian and Greek restaurants have tended to move into the snack bar slot as far as younger consumers are concerned. They also serve quick, inexpensive meals in rather basic surroundings but ones which are rather more adventurous in content.

- *Middle range conventional*. This is a category which is rather hard to define in exact terms but is used to cover the generality of restaurants in the United Kingdom, and is still fairly significant outside London and the main cities. Typically they serve three- or four-course menus of a traditional British type to a middle-class and often middle-aged clientele. Such restaurants are, however, declining in number because of the disparity between the cost of the service they offer and the price customers of this kind are willing to pay for food.

- *High class/speciality restaurants*. Most observers think that the growth in restaurant trade will polarise round inexpensive fast food and this, its other extreme. In the latter instance that process is being fostered by the publication of numerous restaurant guides and magazine features on quality restaurants. Customers will go a long way and even into fairly unprepossessing areas to seek out real excellence; for instance, Queenstown Road in south London, a long gloomy thoroughfare of crumbling houses and gas works, is the unlikely location of two of the capital's best and most expensive restaurants. The inexpensiveness of locations of this kind can obviously have a dramatic effect on fixed costs. On the other hand, it can be difficult to repeat that recipe for success in the country because of possible difficulties of getting chefs and other staff outside urban areas.

Layout

Despite the difference of approach regarding location which these places call for, they do have some layout strategies in common. Upstairs restaurants without a ground floor rarely work for some reason, though customers will go into a basement, even if there is no floor at street level. Ideally, however, the entire premises should be on one floor, fully visible from the street. The reasons for one-floor planning are obvious: efficiency is greatly reduced if staff have to fetch and carry on more than one level. It is also essential that a restaurant should have rear access for bringing in supplies and removing garbage and other wastes. To try to do this through the customer frontage is courting disaster. Furthermore, having said that it is possible to establish restaurants in insalubrious areas, that is the exception rather than the rule. In general, the physical and economic quality of the environment is a major determinant in success. It is doubtful, perhaps, whether the Queenstown Road restaurants would have succeeded as well as they have done without the general upgrading of south London which has been taking place.

Counting your assets

In acquiring or renting business premises you get what you pay for. Unlike the antique trade, property of whatever age is a well defined market with little opportunity to exercise subjective judgement and with remarkably few bargains. If you do get one it is as well to look your gift horse thoroughly in the mouth. You will probably have to pay in other ways in the form of repairs, a dubious location, planning problems, a troublesome landlord or whatever. You take your choice but in any case you pay your money directly or indirectly. So, when starting out on the course you have chosen — renting or buying — an inventory of your assets and liabilities will be the first essential.

Current value: £

Assets

House
    Realisable contents (antiques etc)
    Realisable personal possessions (jewellery etc)
    Boat/caravan/second car
    Second home

Savings and investments
    Cash at bank/building society
    Unit trust/capital investment bonds
    National Savings Certificates
    Local authority bonds
    Premium bonds
    Shares

Current amount: £

Liabilities

    Mortgage
    Overdraft/bank loan
    Hire purchase commitments
    Outstanding bills
    Other inescapable commitments (alimony payments, school
    fees etc)

Your assets, less your liabilities, will give you a picture of the unencumbered funds at your disposal for your new venture.

Renting or buying premises

You should be able to raise money by borrowing (we shall deal with this in detail in Chapter 4) — but usually at least 50 per cent of the funding will have to be found by you. This means that renting will probably be better than outright purchase. Remember that you will not only have to acquire the premises, but also leave yourself enough working capital for equipment, repairs, legal costs, and general running expenses until the operation gets into profit, which may not happen immediately. Renting will also mitigate your losses if the venture does not turn out to be a success. The fact that a business has not worked is always a negative

15

factor when it comes to selling it. The purchaser is bound to take it into account in the same way as you would do if the building had a structural defect. On the other hand, there is a great advantage to being the freeholder of a successful restaurant and if you want to sell it you will get the full benefit of the capital gain — though you will be taxed on that.

There are reliefs of capital gains tax available if you buy another business thereafter or if you sell and then retire — you should seek an accountant's advice on how to go about establishing that when the eventuality arises. If you also intend to use the premises as a first home you will not be taxed on capital gains arising on the element of private domestic use. Therefore, if you buy a restaurant freehold and intend also to use it as a home, you should establish with your Tax Inspector right away what proportion falls into the latter category. For instance, if 30 per cent of the area is your private accommodation, you will only be assessed for capital gains on the other 70 per cent when you sell.

The other advantage of a freehold is that you need not worry about interference from a landlord about what you can and cannot do. However, this does not absolve you from local authority bylaws which can be just as restrictive. It will be your solicitor's responsibility to make sure there are no covenants which could prevent you from operating the business in ways which you might regard as essential, for instance having late dances or a disco.

Apart from these factors, the most essential decision is not whether to rent or buy but whether to take on premises that are currently being used as a restaurant, or those which are vacant or have been devoted to some different purpose altogether. Acquiring premises that have not previously been used as a restaurant would not generally be a good idea unless you have already had a lot of experience in working in or running a restaurant. The point is that a place that is already being operated as a restaurant will, or at any rate should, have the main essential operational features attached to it (see also pages 64–5). That is to say:

- Front and rear access
- Adequate kitchen and storage space
- Provision of services such as drainage to an adequate level
- Parking space
- Approval from the Environmental Health and Fire Officers
- Clearance from local authority restrictions
- A licence which can be transferred to a new owner.

These are all important matters which have to be organised if you are taking on premises that were previously used in a different way, though above all you will have to get permission for change of use from the local authority and it is by no means automatic that this will be granted. Objections can arise to some of the characteristics of a restaurant, such as food smells or the sound of clients making a noisy exit in the early hours of the morning.

The other great advantage of taking existing restaurant premises is that it enables you to study the history of the previous venture on that site and hence to establish your own chance of success. The crucial features here are:

- *The accounts of the previous business* over a period of three years. You will need to look at these with your professional adviser. The past owners may try to explain away poor profitability on the grounds that the records have been tailored to minimise tax liability. That may or may not be the case but it is difficult for a lay person to establish the truth or otherwise of such claims.
- *The type and pattern of trade*. Referring back to the first section of this chapter, you will need to check that the kind of restaurant you are planning to start is appropriate to the site. Trading patterns are also important, particularly in restaurants. A place that does tremendous business at lunchtime in a business area may be quite dead at night; unfortunately you are paying rent and rates 24 hours of the day.
- *Competition*. The existence of successful competitors is a good sign rather than the reverse. On the other hand, the fact that your potential competitors are doing badly is not necessarily a sign that you will do better. It could be that the neighbourhood is simply wrong for any kind of restaurant operation.

The result of these investigations will also enable you to judge the true value of that vague concept, 'goodwill'. Unless the place has had a really resounding reputation, in which case the question naturally arises why they are selling, the goodwill will not be worth a great deal. Fixtures and fittings and stock can be evaluated more objectively but here again their value should not be taken on trust, and you might have to spend quite a long time looking at exactly what you are buying in this area — and also what you are not buying. For instance, if the atmosphere of a place depends on antiques and other period furnishings, and the owner claims these as his private property and not part of the fittings, you may find you are in for an unpleasant surprise when you come to take the place over.

One reason why an apparently flourishing place is being sold is because the owner is being subjected to a change of circumstances outside his control. These could have to do with planning or traffic schemes for the neighbourhood, and this is something your solicitor obviously should look into closely. They may also have to do with rent or rates. Rates are becoming a crucial factor, particularly in cities where overspending by councils has produced rate rises which have driven firms out of business almost overnight. These affect both rented and freehold properties though rented ones have the further hazard of rent review. If you are renting premises, you will need to check when the next rent review is due, the frequency of reviews thereafter, the basis of appeals against assessment, your liability under repairs clauses in the lease and other relevant liabilities, eg in respect of insurance of the premises.

Whatever your course of action — renting or buying, taking on an existing restaurant or starting from scratch — the process is long drawn out, both as regards the actual negotiations with the vendor and the preliminary research you yourself should undertake. A non-specialist estate agent may not be in a position either to keep you informed when opportunities for suitable premises come up or to advise you on some of the issues we have raised. Unless you are pretty confident of your own abilities as a negotiator, know the area of your search pretty well and have good intelligence regarding the propety market, you might be best advised to go to a specialist agent. One that specialises in the hotel and catering field is Christie & Co. They have offices at 32 Baker Street, London W1M 2BU and they also have branches in several other parts of the country, including Scotland and Ireland.

Franchising

An increasingly popular form of trading and one which removes the guesswork from a good many aspects of starting a business is franchising. It has established a particularly strong presence at the fast food end of the restaurant market. Most people have heard of such franchises as Wimpy and Kentucky Fried Chicken, but there are several others and their number is growing.

The principle of franchising is that the franchise company, known as the franchisor, assigns to the franchise operator — the franchisee — the right to use the name of the franchise, as well as a range of tested operating procedures covering everything from the food to the decor over a given period of time in a specified location in return for a start-up fee and some form of continuing payment. The franchisor also provides a very substantial amount of help in site location and negotiating the lease. In fact, because of the importance and difficulty of finding prime sites, some of the larger franchisors employ their own property specialists. They are in regular contact with the larger estate agents and developers who often prefer to deal with a known name such as that of one of the established franchisors, rather than an individual small business such as a restaurant. Becoming a franchisee could therefore widen your options as far as finding good locations is concerned.

It will also, as we have stated, give you a 'blueprint' for a restaurant operation that has been tried and tested. The principle is that if you run it exactly as the franchisor tells you, you will attain a predicted set of results that will enable you to recover your initial investment over a period of three to four years. The disadvantage from the point of view of the entrepreneurially minded is that you have to follow the franchisor's formula exactly with regard to food, prices, decor, graphics and even the uniforms of the staff. However, apart from that and the fact that you have to make a continuing monthly payment to the franchisor based on turnover, the business is your own. The only other major proviso is that the franchise agreement runs for a given period of time, usually at least seven years, though in most cases it is automatically renewable; and you can sell the restaurant any time you want to though in most cases the franchisor will want to approve the purchaser.

The reason for that is that the strength of a franchise network depends on the quality of the franchisees. In just the same way as with the branches of a conventionally run multi-outlet business, people tend to judge all the franchise outlets by their experience of one of them. Before taking up a franchise you should, among other things, look at other outlets of the same firm, see what you think of them and whether it is the kind of business you would like to run yourself. You should also talk to other franchisees to see whether the claims that the franchisor will inevitably make about profitablity, level of support before, during and after the purchase, and the general quality of the business format set out in the blueprint live up to the franchisor's promises.

Franchising, while it can be cost-effective in taking expensive bumps out of the learning curve of starting a new business, is not, as some people think, a cheap way of starting a restaurant. It costs about the same as starting independently — perhaps a shade more if you include the franchise fee — and, of course, there is the continuing payment. Thus it is important to get proper legal advice on whether the franchise agreement which is at the heart of the transaction places an equal obligation on the franchisor to do what he has undertaken to do as it does on the franchisee to pay for the performance of those services.

There are nearly 100 franchise companies in the food and drink field in the United Kingdom but not all of them are equally sound. In recent years the banks, particularly the Natwest and Barclays, have become very knowledgeable about franchising and you should check out any proposal from a franchisor with them even if you do not need to borrow money. However, in most cases it is advisable to borrow and in that case the banks will lend you as much as two-thirds of the start-up costs of a franchise they approve — provided, of course, they also approve of you as a borrower.

Choosing the form of business

As well as deciding on the kind of restaurant that you want to run and where and how you propose to operate it, you will also need to think about the legal structure within which you will be trading. This will determine your relationship with the tax authorities, with anyone who is going into business with you, and with anyone whom you are approaching for funds.

Sole trader
As a sole trader your position is the same as that of a self-employed person. The net profit of your business is taxed as personal income and you can claim the same deductions as any self-employed person taxed under Schedule D. Operating on this basis you may also set off any losses you make in the first three years of the business against earnings in the preceding four years and thus reclaim some of the tax you paid before.

There is no obligation to keep audited records and books of account, though obviously you would be advised to do so for normal commercial reasons as well as to substantiate income and expenditure to the taxman. The most significant point to bear in mind while operating as a sole trader, though, is that you will be personally liable for all the firm's debts.

Partnerships

Most of the above points are also true if you should set up in part-nership with other people. As with sole traders, there are very few legal restrictions on partnerships but because all the members of a partnership are personally liable for its debts, even if these are incurred by a piece of mismanagement by one partner which was not known to his or her colleagues, the choice of a partner is a step that requires very careful thought. So should you have a partner at all? Certainly it is not advisable to do so just for the sake of hav-ing company because unless the partner can really contribute something to the business you are giving away a part of what in time could be a valuable asset to very little purpose. Thus your partner should be able to offer either money or expertise which you could not afford to hire.

Dissolving a partnership is a painful affair which quite often means the death of the business they set up together. Thus personal factors as well as commercial constraints should be borne in mind; and whatever you do, even if you go into partnership with your wife or husband, you should get a solicitor to draw up a formal deed which sets out the procedures for the way in which the profits are divided, limits on expenses by any one partner, what happens if one of the partners withdraws for whatever reason and who is responsible for what aspects of the business and what happens if irreconcilable differences arise.

Limited company

The chief advantage of a limited company is that in law it has an identity distinct from that of the shareholders who are its owners. Consequently if a limited company goes into liquidation the claims of the creditors are limited to the assets of the company. It is not difficult to form a company — a solicitor can organise the formalities for £200 or so — but you will then have to operate within a much more formal structure than the sole trader or part-nership. You will have to prepare a set of accounts annually for the Inspector of Taxes and these have to be audited, normally by a qualified accountant. The auditor has to certify that they present a 'true and fair picture' of the company's finances and must make an annual return to the Registrar of Companies which includes, among other things, a profit and loss account over the year and a balance sheet. The company also has to hold properly constituted meetings at which minutes have to be kept which are legally binding on the directors when they relate to decisions.

The limitation of liability is useful if you think you are going to have a substantial number of creditors; certainly if you think you might not be able to pay them at some point! But the banks who are likely to be your principal creditor have taken care of this loophole by demanding personal guarantees from shareholders which override their limited liability. Furthermore, since the company is a legal entity distinct from the shareholders they are taxed as employees of the company under Pay As You Earn (PAYE). This is generally thought to be less favourable to the individual than a Schedule D assessment even though, of course, personal expenses can to some extent be set off against the company's tax liability.

Setting up a limited company from the start is no longer as popular as it used to be because many of the advantages of incorporation have been eroded. However, where a business reaches very high levels of profit its corporation tax liability may be lower than if those profits were attributed to individuals and taxed as personal income. In that case your accountant would probably advise incorporation and indeed in all matters appertaining to tax you would be advised to seek professional advice. It is said that the person who acts as his own lawyer has a fool for a client, and this is true of tax as well as other areas of professional advice where the complexities are increasingly beyond the reach of lay people who also have to run the business.

Chapter 3

Professional Advisers and Consultants

We have already touched on the importance of the role that professional advisers, particularly accountants and solicitors, are going to play in the formation of your business, whether it is to be a limited company or have some other legal status. You will be using their advice quite frequently in matters such as acquiring premises, looking over agreements, preparing a set of accounts or advising you how to keep your books and look for possible signals that call for remedial action on costs or prices. Obviously, therefore, how you choose and use these advisers is a matter for careful thought.

Making the right choice

Many people think that there is some kind of special mystique attached to membership of a profession and that any lawyer or accountant is going to do a good job for them. The fact is, though, that while they do have useful specialist knowledge the competence with which they apply it can be very variable. A high proportion of people who have bought a house, for instance, can tell you of errors and delays in the conveyancing process; and some accountants entrusted with their client's tax affairs have been known to send in large bills for their services, while overlooking claims for legitimate expenses that were the object of employing them in the first place.

So do not just go to the solicitor or accountant who happens to be nearest; nor should you go to someone you only know in a social capacity. Ask friends who are already in business on a similar scale, and if possible of a similar nature to your own, for recommendations. (If you already have a bank manager you know well, he may also be able to offer useful advice.) The kind of professional adviser you should be looking for at this stage is not a big office in a central location. He will have bigger fish to fry and after the initial interview you may well be fobbed off with an articled clerk. Apart from that he will be expensive, for he has big office overheads to meet. On the other hand, a one-man operation can create a problem if the one man is ill or on holiday. The ideal office will be a suburban one, preferably close to where you intend to set up business because knowledge of local conditions and personalities can be invaluable, with two or three partners. Apart from that, personal impressions do count. You will probably not want to take on an adviser who immediately exudes gloomy caution, or one who appears to be a wide boy, or somebody with whom you have no rapport. Some people recommend that you should make a short list of two or three possibles and go and talk to them before making your choice.

What questions do you ask?

Obviously, later on you will be approaching your adviser about specific problems, but at the outset you and he will be exploring potential help he can give you. Begin by outlining the kind of restaurant you intend to set up, how much money you have available, what you think your financial needs are going to be over the first year of operation, how many people are going to be involved as partners or shareholders and what your plans are for the future. An accountant will want to know the range of your experience in handling accounting problems, how much help you are going to need in writing up the books and he will advise you on the basic records you should set up. Ask his advice on your year end/start; this does not have to be 6 April to 5 April, and there may be sound tax reasons for choosing other dates. He may even be able to recommend the services of a part-time bookkeeper to handle the mechanics; but this does not absolve you from keeping a close watch on what money is coming in and going out.

A solicitor will also want to know the kind of restaurant you want to establish and your plans for the future. But he will naturally concentrate on legal rather than financial aspects (so do not go on about money) — he is a busy man, and this is only an exploratory visit. He is interested in what structure the operation is going to have and, in the case of a partnership or limited company, whether you and your colleagues have made any tentative agreements between yourselves regarding the running of the firm and the division of profits. He will want to get some idea of what kind of property you want to buy or lease and whether any planning permissions have to be sought.

How much is he going to charge?

This is rather like asking how long is a piece of string. It depends on how often you have to consult your adviser, so it is no use asking him to quote a price at the outset, though if you are lucky enough to have a very clear idea of what you want done — say, in the case of an accountant, a monthly or weekly supervision of your books, plus the preparation and auditing of your accounts — he may give you a rough idea of what his charges will be. Alternatively he may suggest an annual retainer for these services and any advice directly concerned with them, plus extra charges for anything that falls outside them, like a complicated wrangle with the Inspector of Taxes about allowable items.

An annual retainer is a less suitable way of dealing with your solicitor because your problems are likely to be less predictable than those connected with accounting and bookkeeping. A lot of your queries may be raised, and settled, on the telephone: the 'Can I do this?' type. Explaining that kind of problem on the telephone is usually quicker and points can be more readily clarified than by writing a letter setting out the facts of the case (though you should ask for confirmation in writing in matters where you could be legally liable in acting on the advice you have been given!). However, asking advice on the telephone can be embarrassing for both parties. You will be wondering whether your solicitor is charging you for it and either way it could inhibit you from discussing the matter fully. You should, therefore, check at the outset what the procedure is for telephone enquiries and how these are accounted for on your bill.

A guide — not a crutch

For someone starting in business on their own, facing for the first time 'the loneliness of thought and the agony of decision', there is a temptation to lean on professional advisers too much. Apart from the fact that this can be very expensive, it is a bad way to run a business. Before you lift the telephone or write a letter, think. Is this clause in a document something you could figure out for yourself if you sat down and concentrated on reading it carefully? Would it not be better to check through the ledger yourself to find out where to put some item of expenditure that is not immediately classifiable? Only get in touch with your advisers when you are genuinely stumped for an answer, not just because you cannot be bothered to think it out for yourself. Remember, too, that nobody can make up your mind for you on matters of policy. If you feel, for example, that you cannot work with your partner, the only thing your solicitor can or should do for you is to tell you how to dissolve the partnership, not whether it should be done at all.

Your bank manager

The other person with whom you should make contact when you start up in business is your bank manager because you will almost certainly want some kind of borrowing facility. The importance of picking a unit of the right size which we have mentioned in connection with professional advice also holds true in this case. A smaller local branch is more likely to be helpful towards the problems of a small business than one in a central urban location with a lot of big accounts among its customers. You might also discuss with your accountant the possiblity of going outside the 'big four', though if all the banks give you a thumbs down there may be something wrong with the way you have framed your proposal. Remember that your professional adviser will not know much about restaurants. You will have to convince your bank that your venture will pay, not just that you are a superb chef. For this reason it is a good idea to ask your accountant to come along to your first meeting so that he can explain the financial technicalities and put them in terms acceptable to the bank.

Insurance

Insurance companies vary a good deal in the premiums they charge for different kinds of cover, and in the promptness with which they pay out on claims. The best plan is not to go direct to a company, even if you already transact your car or life insurance with them, but to an insurance broker. Brokers receive their income from commissions from the insurance companies they represent, but they are generally independent of individual companies and thus reasonably impartial. Here again, your accountant or solicitor can advise you of a suitable choice, which would be a firm that is big enough to have contacts in all the fields for which you need cover (and big enough to exert pressure on your behalf when it comes to making a claim), but not so big that the relatively modest amounts of commission they will earn from you initially are not worth their while taking too much trouble over, for instance, when it comes to reminding you about renewals. Apart from these general points you will have to consider what kinds of cover you need. For a restaurant, the main kinds are:

1. Insurance of your premises.
2. Insurance of the contents of your premises.
3. Insurance of your stock.
4. Personal accident possibly extending also to any personnel. (The four above kinds of cover should also extend to 'consequential loss' if, as a result of some mishap, you have to close for a period of time. Remember you will still have to pay rent and rates, no matter what happens.)
5. Employer's liability.
6. Public liability in case you cause injury to a member of the public. You will also need third-party public liability if you employ staff or work with partners.
7. Legal insurance policies cover you against prosecution under Acts of Parliament which relate to your business (eg those covering unfair dismissal and fair trading).
8. Insurance against losing your licence.

Your broker will advise you on other items of cover you will need. But read your policies carefully when you get them and make sure that the small print does not exclude any essential item.

Insurance is expensive (though the premiums are allowable against tax inasmuch as they are incurred wholly in respect of your business), and you may find that in the course of time you have paid out thousands of pounds without ever making a claim. However, it is a vital precaution, because one fire or legal action against you can wipe out the work of years if you are not insured. For this reason you must check each year that items like contents insurance represent current replacement values and that your premiums are paid on the due date. Your broker should remind you about this, but if he overlooks it, it is you who carries the can.

Catering consultants and organisations

There are many sources of help open to you, some costing nothing and some very expensive.

Starting with the latter, independent catering and management consultants earn their income solely from the fees they charge for their advice to clients — or they should. Some, unfortunately, still receive retainers from specific suppliers which means that they are not totally objective. This does mean that they may be cheaper but you should be aware of their divided loyalties. The Hotel Catering and Institutional Management Association (HCIMA) can provide a list of its members who are consultants and therefore adhere to its professional standards.

The consultants will advise on any aspect of your business, from its management and financial control to its design, decor and equipment. If you engage a consultant be sure to have a clear understanding of the likely charges, the basis on which they are made and any extras such as travel which can add up to a sizable amount.

Although expensive, a good consultant can save you considerable time and money as well as supplying expertise you do not have yourself so the investment can be cost-effective.

Many equipment suppliers will provide consultancy and advisory services, particularly in kitchen planning. These services are normally free or the costs offset against any purchase you make. Clearly such services are not totally objective in that they will recommend their own equipment but the most reputable firms do use reliable catering experts. The main point to watch is that you are not persuaded to over-equip.

Both the gas and electricity boards have very good catering advisory services which are more objective than those of the manufacturers and they are well worth contacting.

The Hotel and Catering Industry Training Board

The Board has an excellent advisory service for those thinking of starting a restaurant. The HCITB's Small Business Unit has published a number of books and articles. It also operates a consultancy service giving advice on starting up and helping with problems in an operating business. The initial fee is £30 for an hour and grants may be available from the Manpower Services Commission for more detailed work.

The HCITB also runs conferences. 'Stage one' conferences cover such topics as The Lifestyle of a Small Business Proprietor, Raising the Capital, Finding the Business, and Where Now? Speakers are usually people who have taken the steps you are contemplating and can advise on the problems and pitfalls. There are also 'stage two' and 'stage three' conferences lasting three days and eight weeks respectively to help you find the right business and plan the running of it.

HCITB stage one conferences cost around £35 for one person and £50 for two and are held in various parts of the country.

Once you are established, the HCITB has audio-visual material, book reports, research summaries and training packages for both you and any staff on a wide range of basic and advanced subjects.

The Hotel Catering and Institutional Management Association.

This is the professional body of the hotel and catering industry with some 20,000 members, including students, who have passed or are in the process of passing examinations to qualify for membership.

The HCIMA is most relevant for those who do already or plan to work in larger catering units or hotel companies, in commercial and industrial catering, hospitals or welfare services, and its membership requirements of examination success and substantial management experience reflect those areas.

The HCIMA is a good source of help and advice on education and training in catering. It also has advisory services for employment and legal matters although precedence is obviously given to members. Non-members may attend seminars and conferences organised both nationally and locally although a higher fee is usually charged.

The British Hotels Restaurants and Caterers Association

This is the main trade association for the industry. It represents about 10,000 establishments and membership is open to anyone who pays the subscription which is based on turnover. Services include a monthly magazine, entry in the annual *BHRCA Guide to Hotels and Restaurants*, political lobbying on matters of concern including VAT treatment, tax allowances, food legislation and employment matters. The BHRCA also negotiates for its members to provide insurance schemes and personal retirement plans. Other services include advisory services on tax, law, employment, equipment and the supply of signs and notices.

Other sources of advice

Other trade associations and craft guilds concentrate more on the food and wine side of the restaurant business and are a useful way of meeting others who may share your own interests.

Many organisations will give advice on food and drink. This is usually free and often of a very high standard with excellent presentation of ideas and recipes and even support display material. Such organisations include tourist boards for overseas destinations who will provide recipes, themes and promotional ideas; overseas governmental agencies and food producers, such as the New Zealand Lamb Catering Advisory Service or the Dutch Dairy Bureau and our own food producers' agencies such as the Flour Advisory Bureau and the Fresh Fruit and Vegetable Information Bureau.

The HCIMA reference book has a comprehensive list of all of these organisations plus many more and a visit to the Hotelympia Exhibition, held every other year at Olympia in London, will provide further help and advice.

Other advisers and suppliers

In the course of transacting your business, you will probably need the services of other types of people: builders, to maintain and perhaps refurbish your premises; printers, to produce advertising material, menus etc; surveyors and valuers to assess your property, security firms to protect it with alarm systems, and so on. You should apply the same criteria to these as to your professional advisers. Their services should be reasonably priced and the service performed to the required standard. If the service is of a professional nature, the consultant should be a member of the relevant professional body. Even quasi-professionals, such as insurance brokers, should belong to a recognised association which safeguards ethical standards.

Some of the best advice you can get, though, costs nothing. The various local enterprise agencies, of which there are now over a hundred in cities throughout the country, their rural counterpart (CoSIRA, which stands for the Council for Small Industries in Rural Areas) and the various development agencies in Scotland, Wales and Ireland, do an excellent job counselling new enterprises of all kinds. They are staffed by directors and managers seconded from industry and generally have a good knowledge of local conditions and of other local people who can be of help to you over things like property — an important attribute in the restaurant business. Their services are free, as are those of the Small Firms Information Service and the advice of your local chamber of commerce. A complete listing of addresses (except chambers of commerce) can be obtained from Colin Barrow's invaluable *Small Business Guide*, published by BBC publications.

Many advisers and suppliers are listed in Appendix 2.

Chapter 4

Managing the Finances

If your first love is food and looking after people you may not have thought too much about how you will manage and control the business side of your restaurant. You may even prefer not to dwell too much on the 'figures' side — but a glance at the bankruptcy rate for restaurants should convince you that financial management is vital.

When you begin, take the best professional advice for accounting and legal matters; it will pay dividends and start you off in the right direction so that you do not waste time and money later on. Indeed, if you hope to raise capital from the bank or another institution, you will need to produce costs, sales forecasts, budgets and cash flow forecasts to convince them that you are a sound business proposition.

Catering is very much a business where you must look after the pennies. The product — food — is perishable, and so is a seat in a restaurant; if you do not use a seat for lunch on any day that opportunity is gone forever. It is easy to waste food by over-ordering or over-cooking in advance, by giving portions that are too large, by adding an extra ingredient which you hadn't allowed for or by over-estimating how many customers you will have each day.

Catering also involves a large number of small transactions many of them involving cash, so good control of both costs and cash is crucial.

Catering costs

There are three main types of cost you will face and it helps to know the total for each.

Materials — food, drinks, tobacco
Labour   — wages, salaries, staff meals, employer's National Insurance contributions, staff transport, uniforms, bonuses, commissions, service charges

Overheads — rent, rates, depreciation, fuel, repairs, maintenance, telephones, cleaning, advertising, stationery, printing etc.

Materials or food costs will be roughly 30 to 40 per cent of your turnover, depending on the standard of food, the size of portions, how much convenience food you use and the standard of the restaurant.

Labour costs will be 25 to 35 per cent of turnover but if you are doing the bulk of the work, this will be a theoretical figure to some extent. Nevertheless, allow for paying yourself the normal market rate for the jobs you will be doing. Again, the actual level of labour cost will depend on the standard of service, how much skill is needed to prepare and serve the food, and how much convenience food you use.

Overheads will normally be in the region of 20 per cent and net profit 15 to 20 per cent of turnover. In fact, many restaurants produce low profits and many restaurateurs expect no more than to make a reasonable living out of the business. However, it can be disheartening to discover that you could have earned more from your money if you had simply put it in a building society instead of a restaurant, so aim for a reasonable profit figure.

Gross profit (or kitchen or bar profit) is an important figure for restaurants. It is the figure left after material costs have been deducted and it is one of the main tools for working out prices and budgets. It also explains why many customers think restaurants make huge profits when they charge two or three times the normal shop price for food — they forget all the other costs which go into preparing a restaurant meal.

It is also helpful to understand that catering costs, like all other production costs, can be fixed or variable. Fixed costs are those which you will have to pay even if you have no customers — almost all overheads and some staff costs, depending on how easily you can adjust the staff rota.

Variable costs vary in direct proportion to the number of meals you serve — the food and drink, some fuel, some cleaning. This is important because, in catering, the variable costs will affect what discounts, special offers, and price cuts you can offer.

Ultimately you must cover all of your costs, whether they are fixed or variable but, in the short term, so long as you cover your variable costs with the price you charge, anything more is a contribution to your fixed costs. This means, for example, that when you have a particularly slow period or a very slack evening, you could offer lower prices to attract new business and still be better off even though your profit margins are cut.

Breaking even

The idea of fixed and variable costs will also help you to see how many customers you must serve before your restaurant breaks even, as the chart overleaf shows.

The break-even chart can be produced for any period which suits your business but monthly, quarterly or annually will be the most useful.

Your forecast of number of customers, average spend and sales are put on to the graph. Draw in the fixed costs you have worked out, then the variable costs, based on the percentages you have decided. Total costs are arrived at simply by drawing in the variable cost line above the fixed cost line. Where the fixed cost line cuts the sales line is the break-even point. This tells you how many customers and how much turnover you need for the period to break even. Sell less and you make a loss; sell more and you make a profit.

The break-even chart is a useful tool to give advance warning if you are running into problems so that you can change prices, cut costs, or do a special promotion before you discover that you can't pay the bills! As each month goes by you can put the actual figures in rather than your estimates to give you a clear, simple graph of how you are doing.

The chart also tells you by how much and when you can afford to cut a price or give a discount. The restaurant in the chart must serve 4000 customers a month spending an average of £2 each to break even. After that, with all the fixed costs covered, the only extra costs involved in serving more customers are the variable costs. If there is no other source of business at £2 a head, the restaurant could afford to drop its prices to, say, £1.50 a head, which would cover the cost of the food and still contribute to profits.

Pricing

Once you have established your costs and how they behave, you can work forward to pricing. There are two aspects to pricing — market considerations and financial considerations.

You will already have decided the broad price range of your restaurant (see Chapter 2) and the average spend and total sales

Break-even chart

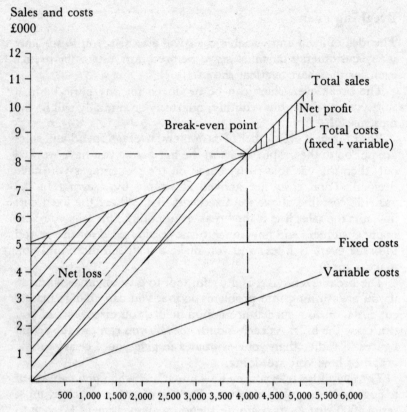

Sales = meals × average spend
Variable costs = food, drink
Fixed costs = overheads, labour
Total costs = fixed plus variable costs

(Chapter 6). The next stage is the financial considerations and the detailed pricing of each menu item so that you cover costs and make a profit.

The aim of pricing is to earn the best profit you can *and* ensure the long-term success of the restaurant. That means giving value for money. People expect certain standards at certain price levels and if you do not provide them, because your prices are too high, you may make a good profit for a short while but only for a short while.

The price you charge depends on:

- The type of customers and their ability to pay
- The menu choice, standards
- How you buy
- The quality of food, cooking, portions
- The quality of service
- The comfort of the restaurant
- Profit targets
- Competition
- The need for growth of the business.

To begin with you may decide to keep prices low to attract custom and become established. If there is keen competition you may have an added incentive for keeping prices down, but it is always best to improve profitability by greater efficiency rather than lowering standards, and by offering something unique or unusual — a unique selling proposition — which keeps you above and ahead of the competition and gives you more chance to achieve the profit margins you want.

Low price does not have to mean low quality and the scope for improving the standard of budget-priced catering in this country is enormous. It is a prime area of opportunity for private restaurateurs with flair, imagination and a good head for business as well as food.

Finding the right price
You may have decided that the average spend in your restaurant must be £10. This could be made up as follows:

Soup	£1.00
Main course	£5.00
Vegetables	£1.00
Dessert	£1.00
Coffee	£0.50
Wine	£1.50

Taking an average food cost of 30 to 40 per cent you can work out the food cost for each item. However, it is usual to vary the food cost from one item to another — on soup, starters, desserts, and coffee the food cost is often only 30 per cent while for the main courses and more expensive items it is usually 50 per cent.

On wine and other alcohol, it is quite common to have a 50 per cent material cost — the price is double the cost — although with the more expensive wines, champagnes etc and for beers, this material cost can be higher, giving a lower gross profit.

Working in percentages is all very well but the final price decides exactly how much each menu item will contribute to sales and costs as the following table shows:

Item	Price £	Materials cost		Gross profit	
		£	%	£	%
Soup	1.00	0.30	30	0.70	70
Steak	5.00	2.50	50	2.50	50
Vegetables	1.00	0.40	40	0.60	60
Dessert	1.00	0.40	40	0.60	60
Coffee	0.50	0.10	20	0.40	80
Wine	1.50	0.75	50	0.75	50
TOTAL	£10.00	£4.45	44.5	£5.95	55.5

If you used a 40 per cent food cost throughout you would find that certain items were priced more highly than customers would expect (eg main courses) and others much lower.

Because the amount of gross profit from each item varies, it helps to forecast how many of each item you will sell. You will also need to do this to buy and prepare the right amount of food (see Chapter 9). This forecast is known as the sales mix and from it you can produce an accurate sales/profit forecast if you want to be more precise than simply working to the 30–40 per cent rule of thumb.

As your experience of the restaurant builds up, you will come to know that on a typical day you will sell 30 steak pies but only 10 steaks and you will be able to calculate the effect on your gross profit of a price change in either item.

Once you have established the food cost for each menu item, you can simply arrive at the price with a percentage calculation.

Because of the previous work you have done in establishing labour costs and overheads, your price for each item will produce the right contribution to these other costs and net profit.

You can also work the whole pricing calculation backwards, starting with the price you want to charge. The net profit, overheads and labour costs are worked out from the usual percentage levels and deducted from the price to give a food cost you must work within. This is very helpful if you offer a standard fixed price menu, for example, or it you have private parties at a fixed price per head.

A la carte menus

These have each item priced separately according to the food cost and the gross profit margins you have decided. If you are pricing an à la carte menu for some time ahead, take care on seasonal items and any increases in raw material costs and build them into the prices you charge. Also be careful not to change the recipe thus increasing the food cost, without changing the prices. And review which dishes don't sell well.

Set menus

Many restaurants offer a set price for three courses either at lunch or dinner. Usually the price of an item on the set menu is less than the à la carte. The advantage to the customer is a fixed price so there should be no 'surprises' on the bill. Portion sizes are usually smaller to allow for the lower prices. Also, the set menu ensures that every customer will have — or pay for — three courses where he might normally have only one or two. The extra volume allows for the lower pricing, on the break-even principle explained earlier in this chapter. But be sure your customers want a full meal or they will resent paying for it.

The disadvantage of the set menu is that you will need to forecast accurately how many of each item to prepare. Customers arriving later must still be offered a reasonable choice yet overproduction will lead to waste.

One way round this is to vary the price of the three courses according to the price of the main dish chosen. This helps to prevent all of the most popular dishes being sold too soon, especially if your pricing reflects popularity as well as food cost.

Daily specials

A dish of the day is a good way of bringing variety to a standard menu or extending the price range of the à la carte menu — at lunch-times, for example, a lower priced dish of the day is very popular. It can also bring seasonal items to a standard menu.

Extras

Service charges, cover charges, additional charges for vegetables and so forth can all boost your revenue — and the shock the customer receives with the bill. Think very carefully before using extra or hidden charges. People do resent them and would much prefer to know in advance the real cost of the meal.

Service charges are increasingly common in many restaurants. In lower priced establishments this may be a fixed sum added to all bills. In expensive restaurants, it will usually be 10 or $12\frac{1}{2}$ per cent of the total bill. Customers are within their rights to refuse to pay a service charge if they wish but this seldom happens.

There is no legal control on how you use the service charge: some restaurants distribute it all directly to the staff, either all of them or just the waiting staff. Others pay a higher level of wages and treat the service charge as part of the normal revenue. Although this might make better economic sense for staff, in practice most catering staff are used to tips and prefer a distribution of the charge.

The service charge must be added to the bill before VAT is added.

Value added tax

VAT must be charged on all food except cold take-away items. Prices may be inclusive or exclusive of VAT so long as this is clearly specified on the menu. When the tax was first introduced many restaurants showed it separately but increasingly inclusive prices are becoming the norm to avoid the shock of a $12\frac{1}{2}$ per cent service charge and a 15 per cent VAT charge being added to the basic prices on presentation of the bill.

If your prices are inclusive of VAT do not forget to deduct it when working out your sales and turnover. (The VAT content of a VAT inclusive price is 3/23rds with VAT at 15 per cent.)

Budgeting and basic accounts

Budgets are simply plans, usually financial plans. The most useful are sales and expenses budgets and the most useful periods to cover are yearly, quarterly and monthly (or four weekly).

A budget gives you a target, a yardstick, against which you can compare your actual achievements. As you prepare the budgets you are forced to think ahead and make decisions about the direction and growth of the restaurant. And the process also highlights any problems which might lie just around the corner — or opportunities.

Budgeting draws together all your previous work on prices, capacity, costs, staff levels, buying and sales volumes. It acts as a check on your earlier calculations and it is an essential item if you want to win over your bank manager.

The first budget is always the hardest because there are so many unknowns. But even when you have had several years of running a restaurant the budget is still only a forecast and may well prove to be inaccurate as the year goes on. This does not matter. The purpose of the budget is to be a plan and to show you where variations occur so that you can pay special attention to them before a problem gets out of hand. Fresh competition may cause a dip in sales, rent increases may mean you need to raise prices, staff costs may have crept up without your realising, wine sales may be dropping because you have overpriced them. A budget will highlight such problems when you compare actual results with forecast, helping you to keep the business on the right road.

Sales budget

This is the master budget for the forecast of sales which will help you to decide the budgets for staff, materials and such things as equipment.

The starting point is the required turnover, worked back to the average spend and the number of customers needed to produce that turnover. These figures can be produced for different parts of the restaurant — the bar, for example — and for different periods of the day.

Sample sales budget for . . . (month)

	No of customers			Average spend			Sales		
	Budget	*Actual*	*Variance*	*Budget*	*Actual*	*Variance*	*Budget*	*Actual*	*Variance*
Restaurant									
Bars									

This will show whether total sales are up or down, whether you are attracting enough customers, whether they are spending more or less than you expected. More frequent budgets will also highlight the sales pattern of your restaurant so that you can pinpoint the peaks and troughs, staff accordingly and advertise or mount promotions to fill in the troughs.

Expenses budget

Because materials costs are directly related to the volume of sales it is not necessary to produce a cost of sales or material cost budget. But overhead budgets are important.

From your initial cost analysis you will have an overall figure for total overheads — say 20 per cent of sales. Within that total certain items will be beyond your control once the restaurant has opened. These items include rent, rates and any interest charges.

Other costs you have some control over and so you can decide how much to spend from the money left over. These include advertising, stationery, entertainment, travelling expenses and insurances.

Finally there are costs over which you have some but not total control — fuel bills, postage, telephone, cleaning, printing, licences, repairs, maintenance, professional services and auditing.

Staff costs will vary to some extent with the volume of sales, but not totally. But it should be possible to work out what staff you need for quiet and busy periods and this will also give you the basis for drawing up staff rotas.

Capital budget

This covers any equipment from deep freezers, boilers and cooking ranges to knives and forks, table-cloths and menu covers. It also covers a vehicle which you may need to get to and from the restaurant at difficult times and to transport shopping.

To begin with you will not be able to afford all the equipment you may want — or think you need — but you should allow for replacements and possible additions as the business becomes established.

Trading account budget

This is a simple statement of sales and cost of sales:

	Budget	Actual	'Variance	
	£	£	£	%
Sales				
Less: cost of sales				
Food				
Bar				
Sundries	_____	_____	_____	
	£			
Gross profit	£	_____	_____	
% Gross profit				

Profit and loss budget

This combines the trading account with the expenditure budget to arrive at the net profit you are likely to make over whatever period you have chosen to budget — again a year, a quarter or a month is the normal period.

Profit and loss budget

	Budget		Actual		Variance	
	£	%	£	%	£	%
Sales						
Less: cost of sales	£	_____	_____		_____	
Gross profit	£					
Less:						
Labour	£					
Overheads	£	_____	_____		_____	
Net profit	£	_____	_____		_____	

Cash flow and cash budgets

These forecast what cash will be available to you to pay bills as they fall due, pay staff regularly, settle VAT and Inland Revenue payments, cover the occasional crisis such as a leaky roof or replacement for essential equipment and, of course, provide you with the money you need for yourself.

A cash budget is vital. Trading profitably is not the same as having money in the bank when you need it and more businesses fail because of this than for almost any other reason. Preparing a cash budget will allow you to see when there may be a shortfall so that, if you must, you can negotiate an overdraft to cover it. You may also be able to alter the date some payments fall due and find the best time to buy new equipment.

Your first cash budget will also identify how much working capital you must provide to tide you over — buy your first stocks, your first equipment and so forth — until the restaurant is producing enough turnover and profit to cover these items.

The cash budget is drawn up for each month to show exactly when each item of expense and sales revenue comes in and how much surplus or deficit of cash there will be each month.

The receipts side is usually straightforward as most restaurants are paid in cash or by cheque as soon as each meal is served. If there are any credit sales — perhaps you have an account for a large company who uses the restaurant regularly — allow for 30 days or perhaps 60 before you receive payment.

If you accept credit cards, check to see which ones pay quickly and which take their time: some can take six weeks. Allow also for the commission payments these card companies charge: anything from 3 to 8 per cent.

On the payments side for some food items you will probably pay cash on delivery but if you use the same suppliers regularly it will pay you to have a credit account which will have to be settled monthly. Suppliers will want to take out credit or trade references if they do not know you. They may also offer trade discounts of $2\frac{1}{2}$ per cent or more for prompt payment which is worth having, but prompt payment of accounts is a good policy in any case. Suppliers soon learn who are the bad payers and either refuse to supply them or do so grudgingly which would not help you to buy well if you were culpable.

Staff must be paid weekly or monthly in arrears.

National Insurance, Inland Revenue and PAYE deductions are payable monthly in arrears to the Inland Revenue. VAT is payable quarterly in arrears to HM Customs and Excise. You may prefer to pay this money, collected on behalf of the government, into a separate deposit account so it is not spent inadvertently. On the other hand, if your cash budget shows that it is likely to be useful to have these funds in your current account, make use of this, so long as money is available to make the payments on time.

Rent is usually payable quarterly or half yearly in advance, depending on your lease. Rates are due half yearly in advance.

Services — gas, water, electricity and telephone — are as for

Cash budget

	Jan £	Feb £	Mar £	Apr £	May £	June £	Jul £	Aug £	Sept £	Oct £	Nov £	Dec £
Receipts												
Payments												
Food												
Drink												
Wages												
Rent												
Rates												
Fuel												
Capital												
Others												
Tax												
Surplus/ Deficit												
Balance from last month												
Balance carried forward												

domestic bills: mainly quarterly in arrears with the standing charge in advance.

Controlling costs

Once you have prepared budgets, it is important to control all costs — that is to check exactly what they are and to compare them with budget and investigate any variance.

The most important area to check is material costs, for two reasons. The first is that food and drink are easy to waste and easy for staff to pilfer. The second reason is that the volume of business — and therefore the costs of materials — is so variable in a restaurant that good cost control is the only way to make sure that you are meeting your targets.

There are five stages at which catering costs should be checked:

Buying
Receiving and storing
Issuing or using
Preparing
Selling

The first four are all dealt with in Chapter 10 because they relate so closely to how you buy materials. The fifth stage involves the control of cash.

Keeping the cash

Most of your sales will be cash sales and you obviously want all of that cash to reach the till and the bank. If you are the only one involved in handling cash then it will, but if any other person is involved, it is vital to have various safeguards against stealing and a whole range of 'fiddles' which can break your business before it gets started.

The controls you put on the cash should also cover the food and drink issued from the kitchen and bar, it is not unknown for kitchen and waiting staff to work together to cheat the owner.

The basic elements of a cash control system are:

1. All items issued from the kitchen or bar must have a chit or order.
2. All cash takings must have a bill.
3. All items from the chit must appear on the bill.
4. The cash/cheques and credit card vouchers in the till (less any float) must equal the total of the bills and the total rung up on the cash register.
5. The money paid into the bank must equal the cash etc in the till.

Each chit and each bill is numbered consecutively so that it is not possible for one to be missing without you knowing. Thus staff cannot take food from the kitchen and fail to put it on the bill. Neither can they present the customer with a bill, take the cash, keep it themselves and destroy the bill.

In a simple restaurant, only one copy of each chit will be needed and the waiter/waitress will write the item on to the bill for the customer.

In a more expensive restaurant the chits are normally in duplicate — one for the kitchen or bar and one for the cashier to use to make up the bill. Such restaurants may also need duplicated bills — one for the customer's copy and one for the restaurant to retain, either as a check on the cash takings or so that an invoice can be raised if the sale is for an account customer.

The till roll or print-out is important and must tally with the total of the bills and the money in the till. This will stop under-ringing (when staff ring up less than the amount shown on the bill and keep the difference for themselves). If necessary you can check each bill against each transaction shown on the till roll.

Automatic machines

Cash registers are becoming very sophisticated with electronic models available which will produce useful information. But they can be expensive.

The simpler electronic register will cost in the region of £500 and apart from the basic cash control information it will also produce a breakdown of the items sold — food, drink, tobacco — calculate the VAT and the gross profit, show which staff carried out the transactions and so forth.

More sophisticated models costing up to £2,500 will also show average spends, sales mix, stock levels, times of transactions, act as a time clock for staff and keep cumulative totals for a week or a month.

Until you know and understand your restaurant and the amount of information you find helpful you may be best advised to use the simplest cash register. After six months or a year may be a good time to review exactly what automated or electronic equipment you would find most useful, you may find, for example, that you want to continue with a simple cash register and use a small computer rather than an electronic machine.

Keeping the books

The legal requirements

If you are a limited company you are legally required to keep books which must be audited annually and to make returns on your results to Companies House and the Inland Revenue. If you are the sole trader or in partnership you do not have to keep books but you must be able to produce financial statements to satisfy the Inland Revenue so that they can decide on your tax liability. If you have a turnover of over £20,500 a year or £7,000 a quarter (1986–87 figures) you must register for and collect VAT and keep detailed records of all transactions.

If you are a sole trader and have more than one business it is the sum total of their turnover which counts for VAT registration and you will have to charge VAT on each one if their total is more than £20,500.

Before you set up a system of bookkeeping, ask your accountant to show you the best and simplest way. After a month or so ask him to go through the books to date to see that you are on the right track. This will also help save time and money when the final accounts and any audit are made at the end of the trading year.

The main books of account you will need are:

1. Cash book
2. Purchases day book
3. Petty cash book
4. Wages book
5. Sales book (if you have a lot of credit account customers).

All the books of account that you will need are available in standard form from stationers and are well worth using.

The cash book

This is a record of all cash and cheques you receive and pay out and payments into and out of the bank.

An example is given here but you can decide exactly which columns are most useful and which analyses you wish to have, according to the information you need. When you buy the books choose those with as many columns as possible: it is far better to have some spare than find you have run out!

Each entry is in date order, giving the total sales for each day or each mealtime if you prefer. On the purchases side, most of the transactions will be individual ones: cheques issued to suppliers, cash drawn out of the bank to pay weekly wages, and so forth.

You may find it helpful to have a 'cash received' book which is simply a daily entry of every bill issued, with its total, its split into food and drink (if you need it) and the VAT. This also gives you a secondary check that each bill is in fact accounted for and it is a simple matter to total each day's bills from this book and transfer the totals to the cash book.

Purchases day book

This is a record of all credit purchases you make, most of which will be for food and drink. As each invoice comes in, enter it in the purchases day book together with the day, the number of the order, if you issued one, the amount, any discounts and, eventually when it was settled and the VAT. Use the book also to check suppliers' statements when they arrive.

The purchases day book should be checked regularly to see which invoices are outstanding so that none is overlooked.

Cash book
INCOME

Date	Description	Total	Meals	Bar	Sundries	Cheques	Credit cards	VAT	Total less VAT	Bank

Bank = money paid into your bank (from the paying in book)

EXPENDITURE

Date	Description	Total	Food	Drink	Sundries	Wages	Overheads	VAT	Total less VAT	Bank

Bank = cheques issued by you in payment (from cheque book stubs)

Petty cash book

You will need to make small cash payments — stamps, fares for staff, cash payments for small deliveries, occasional cleaning items, for example. It is a bad habit to draw this from the till although many restaurateurs do. A petty cash system will ensure that the money is properly accounted for and that you have VAT receipts so that you can claim back the VAT you paid.

The petty cash book is similar to the purchases side of the cash book, with columns for total, VAT, and an analysis of the cost — postage, stationery, travel and so forth.

Each month the petty cash starts with a fixed amount, say £50. At any time the total of cash and chits in the petty cash box should total £50. At the end of each month (or week), the chits are taken out, totalled, each one is entered in the petty cash book and the money in the box topped up to the £50 again. This is known as the imprest system and is simple to operate once you have tried it.

The wages book

You will need this, if you have any staff, to record their pay and the deductions for PAYE and National Insurance. The Inland Revenue will provide all the basic information you need but you may need your accountant to explain it to begin with.

You can buy wages books already ruled up and headed in the right way to show the employee's name, NI number, gross earnings, tax deducted, NI deducted and net wage. It will also show the employer's contributions to NI.

The sales book

You will only need this if you have sales on credit to account customers. As each credit sale bill comes from the cashier, it is entered in the sales book by date order with the customer's name, the amount and the VAT. At regular intervals you should check the sales book to see who owes you money and issue an invoice or statement accordingly. Don't hesitate to send statements as reminders: many large companies are quite slow at paying and if you find this a problem it is worth finding out the date by which your invoice must be submitted in order to be included on the monthly payments sheet.

The balance sheet

At the end of the year your accountant will produce a balance sheet which shows the assets and liabilities of the restaurant.

Assets include premises (either freehold or long leaseholds), equipment, money owed to you by debtors, stocks, and cash at the bank.

Liabilities include the capital you have invested in the business (which the business therefore owes to you) plus the net profit for the year, less the money you have drawn out (if you are a sole trader), money owed by you to suppliers and to long-term lenders such as the bank and any bank overdrafts.

From the balance sheet you will be able to see how much return you have made on the capital you have invested; whether you have a dangerously high level of current liabilities (debts, loans) or whether the level of current assets (stocks, debtors, cash at bank) is enough to meet the current liabilities if necessary. If they are not, you will be trading while insolvent which is illegal.

Finally, the balance sheet shows how fixed assets are valued, so you can check that this is right and the depreciation you are allowing is sufficient to replace the assets when they come to the end of their useful life.

Paying yourself

When all of this financial management is done, there remains the matter of how you pay yourself.

Sole trader
If you are a sole trader your payment is simply the net profit made by the business. You will need to decide how much money you need to draw out of the bank each week or month for your own purposes — making sure that this does not exceed the net profit you expect to make, and enter the amount in the purchases side of the cash book.

When it comes to the end of the year, the final profit and loss account will not show any figure for your drawings — they are not an allowable expense against the profit of the business as far as the Inland Revenue is concerned. Instead, you will be liable for tax on the profit you have made as an individual.

You will be taxed one year in arrears, the exact date depending on when you began trading. If, for example, you started on 30 April 1986 your results at the end of April 1987 will be the basis for tax which you will have to pay in two instalments — on 1 January 1989 and 1 July 1989.

In the first three years any loss you make can be carried back against income from other sources, and taken into account on future profits. You may well find that by the time you have deducted the allowances you are entitled to you will have a book loss.

These allowances include capital allowances for equipment, a vehicle, and so forth. You can also claim expenses incurred when you started but before you were trading and interest other than that paid to the bank.

Your accountant should advise you on all of these matters to make sure you take advantage of whatever concessions you can.

Sole traders are liable for two types of National Insurance contributions: Class 2 is a flat rate contribution of £3.75 a week (1986–87 rate) which you can pay by direct debit or by buying stamps at the post office. Class 4 is an additional payment based on any earnings you have above a certain level: currently this is 6.3 per cent on profit between £4,450 and £14,820 a year (maximum: 1986–87).

For these extra payments the self-employed receive no real additional benefit.

Company director

If you are operating a limited company you will pay yourself as an employee of the company just like any other member of staff. This will be allowed against the net profit the company makes before it is assessed for corporation tax.

You will be liable for income tax on both your salary and any bonus under the PAYE scheme. You will also pay Class 1 National Insurance contributions. The company will have to pay corporation tax in the current year — that is, nine months after the end of your trading year.

Pensions

The self-employed do not fare well under the state pension scheme, despite their extra National Insurance contributions.

As an individual you can pay into a private pension scheme and get tax relief on payments up to $17\frac{1}{2}$ per cent depending on your age. The allowances for a company pension scheme are far more generous and could be one very good reason for deciding to become a company rather than a sole trader.

The whole subject of pensions is increasingly complex with an enormous range of schemes on offer. Expert and independent advice is crucial and it is well worth taking the time to make adequate allowances, especially if you are self-employed.

Raising finance

Restaurants have a big financial advantage over many other forms of small business in that most of their trade is in cash. But start-up costs are high and it is almost certain that you will have to borrow money. Where can you go and how do you set about it? In most cases the banks are the answer but you will have to frame your approach not only in terms of how much you need but also what you need it for and when. The reason is that the banks will see your borrowing requirements not as a lump sum but as a number of packages which have to be wrapped in different ways.

Overdraft

An overdraft is a facility to borrow up to an agreed amount. It is the most common form of bank finance and is used to cover short-term deficits in your cash flow. Interest is payable on a daily basis of actual borrowings, not on the full amount of the facility, at a rate of 2 or 3 per cent over base lending rate. The main disadvantage of overdrafts is that the facility can be withdrawn if the bank manager does not like the look of your financial situation — which is liable to be when you most need the money.

Term loans

Term loans have a fixed period which can range from five to twenty years and are used to finance larger items of equipment or even part of the purchase of the premises; or in the case of franchises, the start-up cost. The duration of the loan depends partly on what the bank considers to be a realistic repayment period. Generally, for larger amounts there is a capital repayment holiday for the first couple of years.

The advantage of a loan is that it cannot be withdrawn but you will need professional advice on handling the interest element which can be either fixed or flexible. If interest rates are low at the time you negotiate them, it may be worth your while going for a rate fixed at the level operating at that time. The reverse is true if interest rates are high at the time you borrow.

As with overdrafts, the level will be 2 or 3 per cent above the bank base rate but the banks will also call for personal guarantees to cover the amount of the loan. In the case of a limited company these guarantees will override the limited liability of the shareholders.

The Loan Guarantee Scheme

If the bank think that you are a sound borrower with a good idea but you are unable to satisfy them in other respects, for instance the personal guarantee, they may advise on approach to the government's Loan Guarantee Scheme which has been set up to cover such contingencies. In this case the government guarantee 70 per cent of the loan to the bank up to a level of £75,000. Interest is $2\frac{1}{2}$ per cent above base rate and the maximum lending period is seven years.

CoSIRA and local development agencies

If you live in a rural area of England, the Council for Small Industries in Rural Areas sometimes act as the lender if they think you are a particularly worthy cause, for instance in creating employment in a depressed area (but would there be scope for a restaurant there?). Alternatively, they will help you put a case for a loan to the bank. The Scottish and Welsh Development Agencies and the Local Enterprise Development Unit in Northern Ireland fill a similar role.

The Business Expansion Scheme

This scheme was set up by the government to encourage investment in small unquoted companies. Investors receive tax relief at their top rate of income tax or up to £40,000 per annum provided they leave their money in for at least five years. However, they must not be directly connected with the business in other ways.

Private loans

Loans are of course different from an investment — a fact that not all lenders appreciate. If you get a loan even from a member of your family, you should have a proper loan agreement drawn up specifying the duration of the loan and the interest and capital repayment scheme attached to it. But you should make it clear in the nicest possible way that the fact that someone has lent you money gives them no say in the running of the business unless the loan agreement specifies otherwise.

If you borrow money from any commercial source such as a bank, they will require cash flow projections (see pages 41–2) and a business plan which sets out the reasons why you think the venture will succeed. That is an approach you should adopt no matter where your funds are coming from or even if you think you will not need any money other than your own. In fact the cash forecast may show that you can get by with an overdraft backed up by hire purchase and/or leasing arrangements. Either hire purchase or leasing can be an effective way of acquiring plant and equipment while leaving your working capital intact. You should, however, shop around before signing any agreement, looking particularly at the factor called APR: annual percentage rate of charge. This can show that what appears to be a modest interest rate conceals a swingeing interest charge as the sum borrowed decreases due to repayments. You should also look at the small print in which nasty disadvantages about maintenance and termination may be concealed.

Cash management
In fact a surprising amount of cash can be kept in the business to cover shortfalls simply by effective cash management. Taking the maximum amount of credit allowed by suppliers while discouraging any attempt by customers to open credit accounts is a good idea. As older style businesses used to say, 'In God we trust, all others pay cash.'

Chapter 5

Employing People

There is a great deal of legislation relating to employment. It affects restaurants particularly because of the high degree to which transient, temporary and part-time staff are engaged in them. There are advantages in employing people in this way because it gives you more flexibility to take on staff as and when you need them, but it does not exonerate the employer from his legal responsibilities. There are, however, certain areas of employment legislation which do not apply to staff who work less than 16 hours a week. For others there are numerous formalities you have to observe.

Contract of employment

The contract of employment statement which has to be issued in writing to every employee who is going to work for you for 16 hours or more per week within 13 weeks of joining is in fact not a pitfall, but a rather sensible document which clarifies right from the outset what the terms of employment are. From the employer's point of view, the necessity of drafting a contract of employment statement should concentrate the mind wonderfully on issues about which it is all too easy to be sloppy at the expense of subsequent aggravation, such as hours of work, holidays and, above all, exactly what it is the employee is supposed to be doing. The following points have to be covered in the contract, and you must say if you have not covered one or other of them:

- The rate of pay and how it is calculated
- Whether it is paid weekly or monthly
- The normal hours of work and the terms and conditions relating to them
- Holidays and holiday pay
- Provision for sick pay
- Pension and pension schemes
- Notice required by both parties
- The job title
- Any disciplinary rules relating to the job

- Grievance procedures.

A further requirement is that employers must issue on or before each pay day and for each employee an itemised statement showing:

- Gross wages/salary
- Net wages/salary
- Deductions and the reasons for them (unless these are a standard amount, in which case the reasons need only be repeated every 12 months)
- Details of part-payments, eg special overtime rates.

Pay as you earn

If you employ staff you will be responsible for deducting PAYE from their wages. The same applies to your own salary from a limited company. The sums have to be paid monthly to the Inland Revenue by the employer.

You will receive from the tax office a tax deduction card for each employee, with spaces for each week or month (depending on how they are paid) for the year ending 5 April. On these cards, weekly or monthly as the case may be, you will have to enter under a number of headings, details of tax, pay for each period and for the year to date. You will know how much tax to deduct by reading off the employee's tax code number which has been allotted to him by the tax office, against a set of tables with which you will also be issued. Without going into technicalities, the way the tables work is to provide a mechanism, self-correcting for possible fluctuations of earnings, of assessing the amount of tax due on any particular wage or salary at any given point of the year.

At the end of the tax year you will have to make out two forms:

1. Form P60 issued to each employee. This gives details of pay and tax deducted during the year.
2. Form P35 for the Inland Revenue. This is a summary of tax and graduated National Insurance contributions for all employees during the year.

When an employee leaves, you should complete another form, P45, for him. Part of this form, showing his code number, pay and tax deducted for the year to date, is sent to the tax office. The other parts are to be handed by the employee to his new employer so that he can pick up the PAYE system where you left off.

Provisions for pregnancy and maternity

The high incidence of women in restaurants makes it important that you should be aware of the employment laws relating to pregnancy and maternity which apply irrespective of married status.

Pregnant women are entitled to take time off work with pay at their normal hourly rate for antenatal care. However, you are entitled to ask for a medical certificate showing they have actually attended a clinic. They are also entitled to return to their former job after a period of absence due to maternity provided (a) that they apply for it not more than 29 weeks after the projected date of confinement and (b) have been employed in their present job for at least two years by the beginning of the eleventh week before confinement, at which time their period of absence can commence. In other words, they are entitled to return after as much as 40 weeks off, though only six of those are paid maternity leave. The employer can claim all of that six weeks' pay through the Department of Employment. In a business employing fewer than five people, the right to return to the previous job in such circumstances only applies if practicable.

Unfair dismissal

Laws relating to unfair dismissal have been relaxed in recent years and they now apply only to staff who have been continuously employed in a business over two years. After that you have to give an employee whom you want to dismiss for any other than a criminal reason at least one written warning — the recommended number is three — that you consider their performance unsatisfactory. You also have to say what they should do to put it right.

You should, of course, be able to spot an unsatisfactory employee within that period but it is a point to watch when you take over an existing business. You inherit its obligations to employees under the Transfer of Undertakings Regulations and these include the provisions of any contracts of employment the previous owners have bound themselves to observe.

Redundancy

If an employee has been on the payroll continuously for two years or more, he or she is entitled to redundancy pay on a formula based on length of service and rate of pay if their job ceases to exist. The statutory payment amounts to a week's pay for every year of service with a maximum of 12 weeks' pay. Some of this money can be reclaimed by the employer from the Department of Employment but potential redundancy situations are another point to look out for in taking over an existing business.

Statutory sick pay

Employers are responsible for paying statutory sick pay for up to eight weeks in any one year after an employee has been sick for more than four consecutive days. These include non-working days, even a Sunday or a holiday. The amount due to them is their gross weekly average wage during the previous eight weeks less tax and National Insurance. The only exceptions to the SSP obligation are employees who have been taken on for an agreed term of less than three months or those who have reached pensionable age.

Employers can recover SSP by deducting it from the Class 1 National Insurance contributions they send to the Inland Revenue. You should, however, be satisfied that there is reasonable evidence of illness. Self-certification is accepted for the first four to seven days, thereafter you should ask for a medical certificate.

The DHSS require you to keep records of employees qualifying for SSP. This has to be done on forms which they supply and they will happily send along an inspector to show you how to do it.

Health and Safety at Work Act, 1974

This is a most important piece of legislation which applies even when you have only one employee though there is an exemption if that employee is a direct member of your family. Even then you would be well advised to observe the Act's requirements and in the case of a restaurant it is unlikely you would get a licence unless you did so. They extend to the safety of equipment, access and exits, storage and handling of goods and structural safety. In a restaurant the state of floors and floorcoverings is particularly important because of intense traffic by staff and customers. Another aspect of special relevance to restaurants is the provision of adequate toilet facilities. If you employ more than five people of different sexes, separate toilet facilities have to be provided; and even if you work entirely on your own you are obliged to have a properly constituted first aid kit on the premises.

Other employment-related Acts

Under the Race Relations Act of 1976, it is illegal to discriminate against employees or customers on grounds of race, no matter what the size of your operation. However, the Race Relations Act does not apply to employing non-British citizens unless they have a work permit — on the contrary, you have to get permission to employ such personnel irrespective of race. The procedures are set out in leaflet OW5 available from PER and Jobcentres.

The Equal Pay Act, 1970 and the Sex Discrimination Act, 1975, make it illegal to discriminate between employees in any way on grounds of sex but it does not apply if you have fewer than five employees.

Chapter 6

The Right Premises

The most important aspect of finding premises — location — has already been covered in Chapter 2. But once you have decided on the type of restaurant you want, whether to buy a going concern or start from scratch and where it is to be, there are many detailed points you must consider in choosing the right premises.

What do you need space for?

The four main areas of space are needed for:

Seating for customers
Food preparation
Storage
Other — including delivery, guest cloakrooms, staff rooms, rubbish, and office space.

Seating

This is the starting point. Once you know how much seating space you need, everything else falls into place. Establishing this calls for a certain amount of advance planning because the seating space depends on several factors and it is at this stage that you must start to make some basic decisions on the type of restaurant you will be running.

The basic unit of production in a restaurant is a meal and the number of seats you have determines your total production capacity. If your dining room is too large you will waste money paying for unused space and be faced with the most depressing sight of all — an empty or half empty restaurant. On the other hand, a restaurant which is too small will not allow you to serve the number of customers you need to achieve the turnover you want. These are the main factors which decide the space you need for seating:

Total sales needed
This is decided by: overhead costs, food costs, staffing costs, and profit.

Obviously sales must cover the total of these costs and leave your profit. You may have calculated these figures for the complete year but at this stage they must be worked out for each period of service so that you have a sales target for each day or each meal period.

Average spend

This is the amount of the average bill, including drinks, cigarettes and any extras. It does not include VAT which is not part of your revenue but the VAT man's. Many a promising business has been ruined by this simple mistake.

At this stage the average spend will be a target figure until you have priced your menu precisely but you should have an approximate figure in mind.

Average service time

This is how long each customer is seated in the restaurant and will vary depending on the style of service. In McDonalds the average service time is probably 12 minutes; at the Ritz, two hours. In a traditional restaurant giving ready plated service 45 to 60 minutes is the norm.

In a self-service restaurant, average service time is about 20 minutes.

How quickly you can or want to serve people will depend on how efficiently you cook and serve, how long you keep people waiting between courses, how and when you present the bill, where you serve coffee and how long they want or expect to stay.

There are various ways of encouraging a faster turn-round — rapid tempo background music, bright lights, a chair comfortable for only a certain length of time. . . in short, the more comfortable you make your customers the longer they will stay which may be fine for an exclusive expensive restaurant but not in a budget one where you need the table for the additional revenue.

These points will not be decided until you design the details but it helps to have them in mind when choosing premises.

Number of sittings

This is determined by the average length of service and the total time of the meal period. Most people want lunch between 12.30 and 2pm so with an average service time of 45 minutes you could, in theory, use each table twice during lunch.

In fact, time is lost in re-laying tables, and space is lost when each seat is not in use — three people at a table for four. Added to this, customers will not arrive on the dot of 12.30 but over a staggered period, giving insufficient time to reuse the table before lunch ends.

All of this means that for many restaurants, only one or one and a half sittings is possible. For faster service restaurants this might rise to two and a half.

Location will also influence the number of sittings. A prime city centre location will mean a longer service period, especially for dinner. A quiet country or provincial town setting will mean an earlier finish for dinner with less scope for a second sitting, unless there is a theatre or entertainment centre nearby.

A word of warning here. If you see over a restaurant which always seems busy, check if the service is slow and the people you see are waiting for service rather than changing over to produce higher sales.

You will not know each of these four variables, but they are closely related, and a realistic assessment of two or three will help you to establish how many seats your restaurant should have.

Basic space calculations

$$\text{Number of meals to be sold} = \frac{\text{Total takings per session}}{\text{Average spend}}$$

$$\text{Number of seats needed} = \frac{\text{Number of meals needed}}{\text{Number of sittings}}$$

$$\text{Number of sittings} = \frac{\text{Total service time}}{\text{Average service time per table}}$$

Example. A restaurant must take £120 each lunch-time to cover its costs and make a profit. Each meal will produce £2 of sales, service will take 45 minutes, allowing one and a half sittings.

To meet its sales target, the restaurant must have 40 seats, to serve 60 people during lunch.

Alternatively, the restaurant could increase its prices to reach an average spend of £3 in which case it would need to serve 40 lunches, using 26 or 27 seats.

Or again, it could speed its service to reach an average service time of 30 minutes to allow two complete sittings at £2 per head which would need seats for 30.

The fine tuning of these calculations cannot be done until the accurate overheads and other costs are known and these will depend to some extent on the space and numbers served. But the figures will be sufficient to guide you in the basic selection of a suitably sized restaurant.

Once you know how many seats you need, other space needs can be found simply. As a rough guide, you should allow:

16 to 20 square feet per person for self-service (including the counter).
11 to 14 square feet per person for table service (medium price).
15 to 18 square feet per person for table service (luxury).
10 to 11 square feet per person for banquets/refectory style.

This allowance covers aisles and work stations but not cloak-rooms, bar or reception areas.

The shape of the room, pillars, doors, awkward corners, will all affect its seating capacity so once you have a restaurant in mind use graph paper and templates to represent tables to work out exactly how many seats are possible. An ideal shape is a rectangle with walls in the ratio of 3:5 and the service doors on a long wall. A space of at least 8ft 6in square is needed for a square table and four chairs in a budget, fast service restaurant. This gives a 2ft 6in table, space for the chairs and room to pass. More should be allowed for a luxury restaurant. Banquettes or booth seats take less space (6ft 3in minimum for four seats).

Main traffic routes should be at least 5 feet wide and the fire regulation authorities will normally specify such routes very strictly.

A good size for a fast service, budget-priced restaurant would be 50 to 60 seats. In a more stylish restaurant where atmosphere is important and the average spend higher, perhaps 20 seats would be enough, although a restaurant much smaller than this tends to be uneconomic unless it is almost a 'one-man band'.

A self-service restaurant must have space for the service counter. Usually this is a simple straight run between 10 and 50 feet long. As a guide, a counter 30 feet long offering a good selection of items including two or three hot dishes will be able to serve 60 to 70 people in 10 minutes.

Allowance of 7 to 10 feet must be given for the depth of the counter, including space for the tray support, the customers, staff behind the counter and back service units.

How big a kitchen?
Most people new to catering are amazed at how small many restaurant kitchens are. Often this is because space is at a premium and the priority is seating space, but it also shows that good layout and planning can make even a small kitchen very efficient.

The key word is efficiency and the kitchen must be large enough to allow production of meals during the peak times without undue delays or customers will suffer and so will your revenue.

The size of cooking space needed will also depend on the type of cooking methods you will use — full traditional cooking to a high standard will need more preparation space than a menu which relies on more frozen and convenience food.

Space for other purposes

Storage space, chilled and frozen storage capacity and delivery space will also depend on the methods you will be using, how regularly you will be shopping and how frequent deliveries will be.

Cleaning and wash-up areas must not be neglected. They should be close to but separate from the main preparation areas to avoid confusion during service and to maintain hygiene standards. Dishwashers are a luxury for small restaurants but worth investigating if space and finance allow.

Space is also needed for staff toilets and changing rooms — although in a small place these often double up.

Somewhere for staff to sit and eat is also a luxury but much appreciated if at all possible.

Finally, there must be adequate space for refuse — a point which is easily overlooked.

The restaurant office

Although an office is a luxury in most restaurants there is quite a lot of regular figure work and it will be far easier to tackle if you have a quiet office or corner away from the main work place.

In the office you will need or find use for:

Telephone
Desk
Adding machine
Typewriter
Safe for cash, floats
Accounting books — cash book, purchases book, petty cash
                              book, wages book
Filing cabinet
Files for: invoices received in date order and numbered
            purchase orders by order number
            invoices you have issued (credit sales)
            cheque book stubs, paying in books, bank statements

budgets
suppliers' names, phone numbers
staff records
VAT returns
Inland Revenue
correspondence
promotion/advertising

Secure cupboard for petty cash box, numbered stationery items.

Allocation of space

The following table gives rules of thumb for deciding on space for each main area of the restaurant.

Area	Percentage of total	Examples	
		30-seater luxury restaurant	60-seater budget restaurant
		sq ft	*sq ft*
Dining	50.0	450.0	660
Food preparation	20.0	180.0	264
Storage	10.0	90.0	132
Cleaning/ wash-up	7.5	67.5	99
Guest cloaks	7.5	67.5	99
Staff WC	5.0	45.0	66
TOTAL	100	900	1,320

Having done all your calculations and used the rules of thumb, don't despair if you find premises which are ideal except for the space and shape of the restaurant. One of the delights of privately run restaurants is their individuality. People have run extremely successful restaurants which defy all the basic rules. The wrong space in the wrong shape doesn't mean that a restaurant is not possible, simply that extra ingenuity is needed in its design and, almost certainly, extra effort in its operation.

Access

Space is one consideration. Access is another. Customers must be able to get to the restaurant — and easily. They will not beat a path to your door. Your entrance must be clearly visible; the more it can be seen the more you will attract 'chance' trade and advertise your presence. It may well be necessary to improve the external access with lights, plants, and good signs.

Ideally, a restaurant should be on the ground floor with the kitchen on the same level to avoid running up and down stairs during service or installing an efficient but expensive lift (dumb waiter).

If a restaurant is above or below ground level customers will resist using it. People like to see where they will be eating.

To overcome this resistance calls for clever desgin of the entrance and stairway. Various reassuring signs must be used to tell people that the restaurant is worth the risk of going up or down stairs. Photographs, good lights, clearly displayed menus, soothing music, decor which encourages, all must be used with care to usher customers to the dining room.

If the dining room must be other than on the ground floor, basements are marginally preferable to upstairs rooms but avoid both if you can.

There should be a rear entrance, otherwise all deliveries and refuse removal must be via the restaurant and, despite all pleas to the contrary, this will be at your busiest times!

The fire authorities will also have a view on access and exit routes and should be consulted at an early stage to avoid a nasty shock if you discover, too late, that you need expensive work done to comply with the fire regulations.

Car parking

Whether you need car parking space will depend on how your customers will get to the restaurant. In a city centre there should be no need but a country location is obviously a different matter. The local authority may well specify the space you must provide.

There must also be access to the back door for delivery vans.

Services

Gas, water and electricity plus good drainage are all needed.

Gas

Most caterers still prefer to cook with gas although there are good electric versions of most equipment available. In particular, cooking hobs are almost always gas. Ovens can easily be electric.

Unless you are planning a very large restaurant, normal gas supplies are adequate but you should consult the local gas board on the best size of pipe to feed gas from the meter to the equipment so that at peak consumption, supplies are maintained at the right pressure.

Electricity

Heating, ventilation, fridges, freezers and smaller equipment will mean a heavy use of electricity at certain times and you should consult the electricity board on the size of supply you need and the tariff which will give you the most economical charges.

In a professional kitchen all electrical fitments must be very strong and designed to withstand moisture, steam etc.

Lighting

The lighting in the restaurant itself will depend on the atmosphere you want to create but in the kitchen there must be good bright light for safety as well as comfort. Fluorescent lighting is invariably used in the kitchen because it uses less power, produces less heat and the tubes last longer than filament bulbs.

Water

Each meal cooked in a restaurant takes between 1 and 4 gallons of water so an ample supply of both hot and cold domestic water is needed. Check that pipes are an adequate size for supply at peak periods and that taps are available where you need them, including potato peelers, dishwashers, preparation sinks, wash-hand basins, in the bar and in the refuse storage area for hosing down.

Hot water at $55°$ to $60°C$ will be needed for washing up and a dishwasher if you have one, and boiling water is needed for tea and coffee making.

Drains

Normal 4-inch diameter drains should cope with the waste water but do check that they are at the right gradient for efficient drainage. You may find that the local authority insists on grease traps because of the extra grease a restaurant produces.

Ventilation and heating

Good ventilation is vital in any kitchen. Waste heat will soon make conditions intolerable and only in the smallest restaurants will natural ventilation via windows be adequate. At the least, roof windows should be installed and a ventilation hood with an extractor over the main cooking equipment to keep the kitchen cooler and stop smells reaching the restaurant.

Kitchen ventilation should provide 20 to 60 air changes an hour in the main cooking area, depending on how large the cooking area is in relation to the size of the room — the bigger it is, the more ventilation is needed. The wash-up must also be well ventilated because of the steam and heat produced. Other areas need only three to six changes of air an hour.

If there is any ducting it must be cleaned regularly — grease-clogged ducts are one of the biggest sources of fires in restaurants.

In the restaurant 10 to 15 changes of air an hour are needed for comfort, depending on the standard of service, whether people are smoking, and so forth.

The greater need in restaurants is likely to be heating especially with people opening doors regularly.

It is possible to buy small air conditioning and heating systems which make use of the waste heat generated in the kitchen to heat the restaurant.

Refuse disposal

Do make sure that there is sufficient storage space for waste, separate from all other storage areas, and that frequent, if not daily, collections can be arranged either through the local authority or through private collectors.

A multitude of legislation applies to buildings in general and catering premises in particular. Further information is given in Chapter 7 on legal requirements.

Premises checklist

- Location: suitability for market
  competitors
  sources of business
  attractions
  views
  traffic
  noise
  suppliers
- Access: customers
  deliveries
  staff
  transport: staff and guests
  car parks
  size of doors
  passageways
  fire exits
- Size: seating area

           kitchen
           storage: chilled
                    dry
                    drinks
                    refuse
           office

- Design: room shapes
  obstructions
  attractive features
  exterior views
  noise: inside and out
- Decor: state of repair
  floors
  fixtures and fittings
- Services: gas
  electricity
  water
  drainage
  sewage
  WCs: staff and guests
  ventilation
  space heating
  water heating
  connection procedures
  refuse collections
- Living accommodation
- Planning consent
- Legal requirements
- Maintenance: premises
               equipment
- Alterations
- Tenure of occupancy
- Date of occupancy
- Rates, rents, other expenses

Chapter 7

Legal Requirements

The licence

One of the advantages of taking over a place that has already been trading as a restaurant is that it will usually already have a Part 4 Licence which allows you to sell wines and spirits with food. However, that has to be transferred to you and it is one of the things your solicitor should look after as part of the handover procedures. He will have to arrange for the grant of a Protection Order to cover you from takeover day until the licence is renewed in your name. This happens annually at a magistrates' meeting. Thus if the place does not have a licence, you will have to wait until such a meeting to get one. Full guidance on these procedures is given in a booklet, *The ABC of Licensing Laws*, published by the National Association of Licensed Victuallers, Boardman House, 2 Downing Street, Farnham, Surrey GU9 7NX. The conditions on which the grant of a licence depends are not only that the premises are run in an orderly fashion, but that a variety of other laws, regulations and bylaws are observed. Thus copies of your licence application also have to go to the Environmental Health Officer, the Chief Fire Officer and the Chief Constable. The main provisions you have to observe are the following:

Cleanliness

Food/hygiene/general regulations. These lay down that raw and cooked food are separately prepared and separately stored under hygienic conditions — for instance that refrigeration and heating plant are properly maintained and that safe storage temperatures are observed. Refuse should be kept in tightly sealed containers and disposed of under controlled conditions. Any infestation of insects or rodents must be treated immediately.

The whole place must be kept immaculately clean, not only in customer areas but also in storerooms and in the kitchen, where surfaces must be kept free of grease and dirt. Furthermore, there must be a cleaning schedule to keep them that way, which includes the regular maintenance of plant for washing dishes and glasses.

There are equally strict hygiene regulations for staff — clean hands and fingernails, frequent changes of working garments, no smoking while handling food, treatment and protection of minor injuries with waterproof dressings. That means an adequate supply of properly equipped wash-hand basins, spotless lavatories and adequate space for storing everyday clothes away from working ones, and of course from food. It is important to get the Environmental Health Officer's advice on the suitability of existing premises and find out what his requirements are on any place you are converting to restaurant use.

Fire precautions

The Fire Precautions Act, 1971. You will also have to obtain a Fire Certificate, FP1, that is granted subject to the Fire Officer being satisfied on means of escape, the provision of fire alarms and fire-fighting equipment, emergency lighting, fire drills and training routines. The Fire Officer pays particular attention to the kitchen because grease around stoves and in ducts is a frequent cause of trouble.

Consumer legislation

There is also a good deal of consumer legislation relating directly or indirectly to restaurants.

The Weights and Measures Acts. These lay down precisely in what volume spirits, beer and cider must be sold. For carafe wines there is at present only a Code of Practice which suggests that these should be served in measured containers.

The Sale of Goods Act, 1979. As the wording implies, this relates mainly to the purchase of goods in shops but one of its provisions is that the goods sold must be 'as described'. This would obviously extend to food and the customer is entitled to ask for his or her money back if it fails to meet this condition — for instance, if the lobster cocktail has been stretched with other ingredients without your being aware of it. (If you wanted to cover yourself you should call it 'seafood cocktail'.) Note that the customer is not obliged to accept a replacement dish.

If you obtain the ingredients readymade from a supplier in all good faith, the onus to fulfil the 'as described' obligations still falls on you. You cannot refer the customer back to the supplier nor can you seek refuge in notices saying 'No refunds' or other illegal attempts to disclaim responsibility for food.

The Trade Descriptions Acts, 1968 and 1972. An honest mistake would be covered by the Sale of Goods Act. However, if you dishonestly describe a dish as being venison when it is in fact horse meat — to take an extreme example — you would be liable for criminal prosecution under the Trade Descriptions Act. Poetic licence, in other words, is definitely to be avoided in writing menus.

The Prices Act, 1974. Under this Act pubs, cafes and restaurants must display a selection of prices for meals and drinks. However, if one of your staff mistakenly prices your Chateaubriand for two at £2 rather than £20 you are not obliged to sell it for the former sum — unless the customer has already paid the bill. Once money has been accepted the bargain has been struck and you can't go back on it. You can, however, point out beforehand that a mistake has been made and obtain the proper amount.

Some parts of consumer legislation are a grey area in the restaurant business. It is difficult for a customer to prove that a dish is not 'as described' if a dishonest chef throws in alien ingredients at the last minute. It is embarrassing to point out to a customer who has already eaten his meal that there was a mistake in the pricing on the menu. In general it is best not to be too legalistic about things and to accept the age-old dictum that the customer is always right.

Chapter 8

Marketing and Selling

One of the biggest mistakes beginners make is to assume that customers will beat a path to their door. They won't. Neither will they come unless your restaurant offers them something they want to buy, which is not necessarily the same as the product you want to sell.

This is the fundamental point about marketing a restaurant just as it is for marketing any other product — you must create, produce and sell a product which people want to buy at the right time, the right place and the right money.

The basic marketing decisions are the location and premises (the 'packaging' of the restaurant) the type of food and the broad price category, all of which have already been considered. The next stage is to get the complete product right.

Getting the product right — the meal experience

The 'product' of a restaurant is far more than the food. It has been called 'the meal experience' because a whole range of factors contribute to eating out and influence a customer's choice of restaurant.

The list of these factors is long and many of them are covered in other chapters. But in looking at marketing and selling a restaurant it is helpful to have a checklist of the factors which influence a customer's enjoyment of the meal. From time to time it is well worth running over each point to see if you have changed any part of your product and how this might appear to your customers. This is really a quality control discipline which it is too easy to neglect when you are bogged down in the day-to-day running of the restaurant. Standing back from the daily routine with the checklist in hand will help you to see your restaurant as customers see it and to correct any faults before they damage your business.

Checklist
- Customer expectations:
  time of day

type of meal
reason for eating out
- Initial impression given:
external appearance
menu displayed
prices shown
access
greeting of customers
- Mood of restaurant:
formal
informal
crowded
spacious
cosy
exclusive
brightly lit
dark
noisy
hushed
- Other customers:
age
sex
size of party
class
compatibility with other groups
- Staff:
skills and ability
age
sex
style of dress
attitude and personality
- Decor:
standard of furnishings
style of decor
table dressings
- Menu:
choice of food
style of cooking
method of description (English, French)
prices — amount and methods of charging
treatment of extras, service charge, VAT
design of menu card
choice of drinks

- Service.
  self-service counter
  buffet
  plated service
  family service
  silver service
  speed
  formality
- Other factors:
  music
  dancing
  entertainment

If all of these main elements of the meal experience are in harmony, customers will receive the meal experience they expect, they will find it good value and they will probably become regular customers. But if one or more factors change — if for example, a budget priced restaurant suddenly introduced a menu in French or a formal, city centre business restaurant began employing young, jean-clad girls to wait on customers, there would be a conflict, and people would begin to be disappointed, although they might not be able to explain why. A regular review will make sure that this does not happen in your restaurant.

Selling your restaurant

Once the product is right you can set out to sell it so that your efforts produce the best revenue.

Many restaurateurs do not actively sell. They rely on reputation, on people finding out about them somehow or other and remaining loyal customers. This can work in the right location; if, for example, the restaurant is in a busy main road where it is easily seen by the many people walking and driving by. But in a quieter location or in the country, you will need to take steps to tell customers where you are, at least until you are established.

Selling techniques will also help to boost profits by producing extra business when you need it most.

Sales patterns
To use sales techniques effectively you must first understand your pattern of sales. Every restaurant has busy and slack times and this pattern has a daily, weekly and annual cycle. Once you have identified your slack times when you want extra business, you can work out a sales strategy.

Daily

Generally speaking the periods immediately after opening are quiet, building up to peak periods around the main mealtimes and then falling again. Sometimes it is useful to have quiet periods so that staff can concentrate on preparing for the busy periods but once service staff are on duty it is most profitable for them to be fully occupied serving customers. Restaurants which are open all day find mid-morning and mid-afternoon the periods which benefit most from some form of sales promotion.

Restaurants which depend on one main source of business may have very slack lunch periods or very slack dinner periods, depending on whether they serve the business community, shoppers, office workers or the evening leisure trade. In this situation the sales target is to build a second source of business which will not conflict with your main source and help fill the quiet times.

Weekly

As a rule, restaurants are quieter at the beginning of the week, building up to their busiest at the weekend. Many restaurants close on Sunday and Monday for this reason. The pattern is more pronounced for restaurants in the evening than lunch-time.

Market days, early closing days and late shopping hours will affect restaurants serving shoppers.

The weather can also make a difference — cold wet weather is often bad news and even a sudden heatwave can cause a slump.

Yearly

Restaurants in tourist areas have the strongest seasonal business with their peak in the main summer months, despite the growing trend to short winter breaks. Conferences may help redress the balance if the town has the right facilities, but not all have.

In a strongly seasonal location, such as Cornwall, it may well be uneconomical to stay open outside the main tourist season.

Year-round restaurants usually find January and August quiet months with December one of the busiest.

Once the restaurant is established, it is wise to keep a diary of sales. A daily note on the number of lunches and dinners, the best-selling dishes, the types of customer, perhaps how they knew about the restaurant, any special points which influenced business.

This will build into a useful sales history from which you can follow trends and draw up a plan of campaign to tackle any problems.

Sales techniques

Make the most of your existing custom

Even quite a small increase in the amount each customer spends will make a noticeable improvement in your profits, so the in-house sales effort is important yet many restaurateurs overlook it.

First and foremost the most powerful sales weapon at your disposal is the food itself. Attractively presented and displayed it will sell itself far more effectively than anything else. This is why many restaurants have a well lit table prominently displaying special dishes, appetisers, desserts, wines and so forth. The principle works just as well in a simpler restaurant. Even a self-service counter can be attractively displayed, as some of the motorway service restaurants have proved, by replacing intimidating stainless steel counters with island displays of well-arranged food.

Second in your sales armoury is the menu. This must be attractive, clear, easy to read and understand, and honestly priced. There should be no hidden extras to boost the bill. Menus range from large illuminated wall panels showing each dish in full colour (Wimpy bars, pizza houses) to hand-written blackboards on mobile easels or even a complete window-sized menu with the choice written across the glass in white script (the Bistingo chain in London has used this gimmick for nearly 20 years with great success).

From across the Atlantic comes news of a computer terminal on each table which not only shows the menu but takes the order and carries out market research on customers while they wait for their meal.

More commonly, menus are printed on cards of all shapes, sizes and designs — not all of them legible or styled to help customers make their choice — which can easily result in a loss of custom, so make sure your menu sells for you.

Third on the sales list are the service staff. Apart from a friendly, welcoming and helpful attitude, staff can boost sales considerably by asking the right questions at the right time, and they should be trained to do this automatically.

Aperitifs, starters, extra vegetables, desserts, wines, coffee, liqueurs, brandies, cigars: all are potential sales yet not all restaurants make sure that every customer is offered each item.

Slow or inefficient service can lose sales: customers may simply run out of time or patience if service is too slow. Over-rapid service, with the offer of dessert too soon after the main course can also lose a sale.

Changes and novelties will keep your restaurant interesting to its customers so introduce new dishes, new ideas, slight changes to the displays and the table decorations. And use point of sale literature to draw attention to the changes. Table cards, a bulletin board by the entrance, a discreet poster in the window will all work for you.

Don't forget that the busy executive who uses your restaurant at lunch-time is also a family man who may eat out in the evening. And the shopper may not realise that your restaurant is quite different in the evening when the lights are dimmed, pretty cloths are on the table and the music is soft.

Finally, there is one big don't — don't oversell or push customers into ordering items they don't want. They may give in gracefully at the time but you won't see them again.

Opening events

Selling to existing customers is a good start but to create new business, fill up the quiet periods and expand your reputation, external promotion is needed.

The first and best opportunity is when you open for business. Whether you have a new or an ongoing restaurant it will be of interest and the changes will give a good focal point for any advertising, entertaining or other promotion you decide upon.

An opening party is appropriate for expensive restaurants especially if the clientele will be from local industry and business circles. Draw up an invitation list which covers local opinion formers as well as the main potential customers. This includes the press, senior marketing and sales people, advertising agents, travel and estate agents, bank managers and leaders of industry. In a large town it is a good idea to invite taxi drivers to a separate party, perhaps a breakfast buffet, so that they know where to find you. It is also good public relations to invite your neighbours.

If you do not want a full-scale opening party, an invitation to cocktails on a choice of evenings is an alternative.

Whatever you choose, don't overlook how tired and pressurised you will be during the actual opening. This and the teething troubles which always arise make a party a few weeks after opening a wiser schedule than a first day event, when you will have more than enough to cope with.

For the most important potential customers, you may want to give individual invitations to lunch or dine with you. This is very effective but very time-consuming, especially if you are chief cook and bottle-washer, so make sure you can be spared for the complete mealtime.

For lower-priced restaurants an opening party may not be feasible because your potential customers will be less easy to identify and reach with a personal invitation. In these cases, it would be better to go for a wider approach: handbills and posters distributed to various local shops, offices and industry will spread the news of your new venture. You may make an introductory offer to encourage trade in the first week or month — this is covered in more detail in the next section.

Large or small, expensive or budget priced, make sure you tell the press of your opening and consider advertising as well.

Discounts and special offers

Money off, free offers and other discounts can be very effective in boosting trade but they need to be carefully planned and well thought out or you could simply be cutting your prices to an uneconomical level without getting any long-term gain.

First, work out the costs very carefully. Can you really afford to offer a free hamburger in a newspaper ad? What if everyone takes up the offer? Should you restrict it to certain times of the day when the restaurant would normally be empty and your tables going to waste? How long should the offer be valid?

The best promotions are self-financing. Any discount you offer should produce enough extra customers so that the increased volume of sales covers the reduced profit margins as well as the costs of mounting the promotion — any advertisements, special printing, extra staff and so forth.

Most restaurants prefer to offer a 'value added' promotion rather than money off — a free glass of wine with a meal, one meal in ten free for special groups or a complimentary birthday cake for celebration parties.

Whatever the offer it should appeal to the customers you want to attract and it should help meet your sales objective and your financial objective. If it does not satisfy these three points, you will be disappointed with the results.

Special events

This covers a whole range of ideas which can boost business and keep your restaurant interesting for customers.

Seasonal menu changes and special dishes to take advantage of new season items are the most common. An extension of this is a special theme to mark dates such as St Valentine's Day, Wimbledon, Hallowe'en, Easter, Mothering Sunday and so forth. Themes based on a particular type of food are also used; a French restaurant might concentrate on one area of the country, with regional dishes, wines and decorations.

These promotions can be effective but they can also become expensive. They take considerable time to organise and research, you may need new recipes and new suppliers, special menus, decorations and props and promotional material to tell people of the event.

Unless the promotion produces sufficient extra business to cover the costs, you will be losing money and you may also lose one or two customers who are disappointed in the change. But if you are satisfied and you think your customers will appreciate the novelty, festivals can be great fun and a good publicity aid.

As well as your own special events, there are those of your customers: birthdays, anniversaries, special celebrations all give you an opportunity to sell your services with a nudge at the right time, in the shape of a table card advertising your special birthday or anniversary cakes, the free champagne cocktail or whatever other promotion you have created.

Christmas is the biggest 'special event' of all and well worth dressing up for. Offer a Christmas party menu and promote it well in advance with handbills, posters and an advertisement as well as table cards.

Public relations
Broadly speaking, many of the activities already covered could be classed as public relations but for the purpose of this section, public relations can be taken to mean press relations.

The most important press for you will be the local newspaper(s), regional or county magazines and if you are at the top end of the market or very fashionable, one or two of the glossy magazines like *Vogue* and *Harpers & Queen*.

At its simplest, press relations involves no more than letting the press know when something newsworthy happens; a new chef, a change of menu, an unusual recipe, a celebrity visit, arrival of an unusual wine or food, a record charity collection, a special achievement or an unusual hobby of your staff and, of course, special promotions and events.

Once you have identified a news story, either write a short, straightforward account of the facts and send it to the editor, or, if you prefer, simply telephone. You will soon find out if the story is interesting enough.

If you want to go further you could offer a regular recipe advice article for the women's page or volunteer comments on local events which affect your business — changes in local tourism policy or traffic changes or rate increases. Once the press know that you are prepared to talk to them they may well approach you for reactions, but don't be too outspoken: you could upset your customers!

Advertising

This can be expensive so you must calculate whether it is worth the expense of telling the right people — potential customers — about your restaurant and encouraging them to patronise it.

Advertising will only work if it is read by the people you want to reach so make sure that the circulation of the media you are considering matches your market. Don't advertise in the local Chamber of Commerce Guide if you appeal mainly to tourists or shoppers. Don't advertise in an expensive national newspaper or magazine if your main business comes from local business people.

For most restaurants, the local newspaper and perhaps a regional or county magazine will be the most suitable place to advertise.

The second rule of advertising is to make sure your ad is seen and read. That means good, strong graphic design so that the ad is highly visible 'on the page'. It also means an eyecatching headline which makes a strong selling point.

Give people a good reason why they should use your restaurant: 'the best romantic restaurant in town for that special occasion' 'the new meeting place everyone is talking about' or 'good food which won't break the bank'. Pick out a point which makes your restaurant different from others — a unique selling proposition — and remember that what you say must be honest and fair.

Most publications have advertising staff who will help you design and lay out an ad but if you plan to advertise regularly it would be worth using a professional designer.

Advertising prices can be negotiated in your favour. Do ask for a discount as a new advertiser or when booking a series. They can only say 'no'. It's also worth asking for your ad to be 'facing matter' — opposite editorial stories rather than other ads. Ideal spots are on the leisure and entertainment pages which are read by people most likely to eat out.

Once you have advertised, try to find out how effective it has been. Ask new customers how they came to know of you. You will never know exactly what impact your ads have but this should give you some indication.

Direct mail

The most valuable use of direct mail is to write personally to important, regular or potential customers telling them about some new offer or service you are providing.

The success of any direct mail campaign depends on the mailing list. It should be accurate, up to date, and include the name of the right person.

The mailing list need not be long but it should be precise. Don't waste time and money writing to people unless you are reasonably certain that they are potential customers.

To begin with, you can research the names and addresses of perhaps the marketing executives in local firms nearby. It is possible to buy the lists of local ratepayers; choose the streets with houses likely to belong to the people you want to serve.

Once you have a list, a good initial mail shot is a simple short letter together with a miniature of your menu. As you become established you may have more names to add, drawn from cheque payments, perhaps. Or you might invite people to give you their full names and addresses so that you can send them details of special food festivals.

If your restaurant is lower priced, it will be more appropriate to have a leaflet drop — a simple handbill, distributed door to door by local newsagents with the normal deliveries. Again, you can select which areas suit your market.

The guides and how to get into them

There is no doubt that an entry in one of the restaurant or food guides can bring you business. Some restaurants have been inundated with new customers as a result of an entry. Others have lost their new clientele almost as quickly when they lost their entry. The people who buy the guides can be fickle but most restaurants decide that the rewards are worth the risks and usually only the most confident restaurateur would disdain an entry.

The most respected guides are the AA guides, Egon Ronay's, Michelin and the *Good Food Guide* from the Consumers' Association. They vary in their criteria for entry. Most subjective is the *Good Food Guide* which asks members to recommend restaurants before they are considered and inspected. Others may accept your request for an inspection if you have been established long enough, usually at least a year.

You will not know if your restaurant has been inspected until it is too late! The inspector may introduce him- or herself after the meal and a practised eye may spot the unknown, solitary figure and guess at the reason for the visit.

If you are given an entry you will know that you have arrived and that a completely independent expert considers that you are doing a good job. The standards set are exacting and only the places which come up to scratch get in, so make sure you have ironed out any shortcomings before you invite an inspection.

Chapter 9

Food and Drink

The food and drink is, of course, the most important part of your product. It is also the part in which you should be most interested. After a long, hot, busy day in the kitchen or restaurant you may never want to see another meal again. Your own dinner may be a boiled egg or beans on toast, because nothing else whets your appetite after being surrounded by food all day. To withstand this pressure you must have more than a passing interest in this fundamental part of your business.

Handling food and drink for a restaurant involves far more than simply cooking and serving. Even a moderately sized restaurant may spend £150,000 on food in a year, so how you buy and handle it can be crucial to your success or failure.

The choice of food

From your basic ideas on the food you will offer, you must devise a full menu and from that, decide exactly what food you must buy, where from, how often, and so forth. The menu is the master plan.

The menu should reflect your own preferences and your cook's skills but beyond that, it must meet the demands of your customers by offering a range of prices within the average spend that you have budgeted. The menu must also offer a reasonable choice and most people will want to see some adventurous dishes on the menu although, ironically, they will probably play safe in their choice — the most popular restaurant meal in Britain is still prawn cocktail, steak and chips and fruit pie or ice cream.

Once customers have confidence in your food they will probably become less conservative in their choice so you must allow for their wish to try something new or choose an old favourite, depending on their mood. Allow for as broad a range of tastes as you can — meat, fish, pasta, plain and elaborate dishes. In this way you will keep your appeal broad as well. Cater for minorities if you have the scope; vegetarians are increasing in number, more people are cutting down on fat, there is growing awareness of

83

additives in food. Cater for such trends and you will be appreciated.

The menu must reflect the equipment you have available. If you are short of oven space, don't concentrate all the menu items on dishes which demand it. Calculate the capacity of the deep fryer before you restrict your choice of vegetables to chips or croquette potatoes.

Another factor is the amount of advance preparation each menu item needs. Ideally, you should aim for a good balance between more elaborate dishes you can prepare partly or totally in advance and simpler items which can be prepared quickly from stock. This will spread the work load, help to prevent bottle-necks on equipment and get you out of difficulties if you underestimate the portions of the pre-prepared food.

Finally, don't be too ambitious — an over-long menu with too many choices will only confuse customers and raise doubts in their minds about whether the food is fresh or all deep frozen. It will also give you problems of storage and stock rotation because less popular items will sell very slowly.

To overcome this problem, design your menu so that the uncooked food which does not sell one day can be used in a made-up dish the next. And offer dishes which make the best use of ingredients rather than wasting one part of, say, the chicken, or the offcuts from the beef.

Menu planning checklist
- Your personal preferences
- Cooking skills available
- Equipment capacity
- A range of prices
- Plain food
- Adventurous food
- Advance preparation dishes
- Instant preparation dishes
- Dishes from leftovers
- Minority tastes
- Broad appeal
- Good choice of textures, flavours, basic ingredients

Testing recipes

Once you have decided which dishes to offer it is wise to test each recipe even if you know exactly what methods and ingredients you plan to use. This is important for several reasons:

1. It will give you a standard recipe for you and the staff to work to.
2. Customers will be given a consistent product.
3. You will be able to check the food cost exactly.
4. You will be able to test different ingredients and different qualities.
5. You will be able to specify more accurately the raw materials you will buy.
6. You will be able to test the yield of each batch of ingredients.
7. You will be able to decide on portion sizes for each item.

Each of these points is very important. Particularly, you will need to establish the waste on items both in preparation and in cooking. For example, joints of beef can lose up to 50 per cent of their weight during roasting but foil wraps will cut this by 10 to 15 per cent, and allowing the meat to rest for 10 minutes before carving it could save another 5 per cent.

With such an expensive commodity as meat you will want to find out the most economical way of achieving the right quality — you may want to do your own butchery or you may prefer to buy pre-portioned cuts of meat which save time and give you a precise cost per portion without the relatively unknown factor of wastage during butchery, thus justifying the higher cost.

The only way to establish the best way of buying food is to test the alternatives.

Portions

Equally important is to decide on portion sizes. Unless you do you will not be able to control the food cost accurately and customers will not be pleased if one gets a large portion and one a small! Haphazard portioning also makes it very difficult to prepare the right number of portions in advance.

Portion size guide

Portions will vary considerably depending on the style of restaurant and its prices but the table below gives some guide.

Soup (cooked)	7fl oz	200 ml
Pâté	$1\frac{1}{2}$–2oz	40–55 g
Fruit juices	4fl oz	100 ml
Prawns, shelled (cocktail)	2oz	55 g
Pasta (dry, uncooked)	2–4oz	55–110 g

Rice (dry uncooked)	1–2oz	28–55 g
Fruit cocktail starter	2–3oz	55–85 g

(All fish, meat and vegetables are raw, trimmed, ready for cooking weight.)

Fish fillet	4–6oz	110–170 g
Fish, bone-in	8–10oz	225–280 g
Poultry fillets	4–6oz	110–170 g
Poultry bone in	8–12oz	225–340 g
Steaks	5–9oz	140–255 g
Stews, casseroles, made-up dishes {	4oz meat	110g
	4oz vegetable/garnish	
Roast meat, boned	4–5oz	110–140 g
Roast meat, bone in	8–10oz	225–280 g
Chops	8–10oz	225–280 g
Liver, offal	4oz	110 g
Potatoes	4–6oz	110–170 g
Green vegetables	5–6oz	140–170 g
Root vegetables	4–6oz	110–170 g
Ice cream	2–4fl oz	55–110 ml
Fruit salad	4–6oz	110–170 g
Cream	1oz	28 g
Pies, gateaux	work on portion per unit, eg 8 per dish, 32 per tray	

To achieve good portion control, you will need standard-sized scoops, ladles, serving dishes, plates, bowls and so forth, because during service you and your staff will not want to measure accurately, you will fill a dish or glass to a certain, easy-to-identify level, or you will give one or two ladlefuls.

On more and more items restaurants are offered pre-portioned packs by catering suppliers. These are convenient; they are also expensive, compared with bulk ingredients on an ounce-for-ounce basis but they come into their own when wastage is taken into account. However, many customers do not like prepacked cheese, butter, milk, cream, jams or biscuits so you must decide whether such items fit your image.

When you have tested and costed all your menu items — including all the small things you would normally overlook such as cooking oil, herbs and stock which soon add up in catering-scale recipes — you can check back to the prices and the portion sizes to make sure that everything is consistent and correctly costed and priced.

You can also plan your buying in greater detail but before

you know precisely what to order, you will need a clear idea of how many items you will be serving: in other words, a volume forecast.

Volume forecast

This is simply the best estimate you can make for the number of each item on the menu which you will sell in a mealtime, a day or a week, depending on which period suits you best.

There are several things to help you:

The sales history

To start with you will not have any record or experience to help but if you keep a check on how much of each item you sell each day the records will soon build up. You will find that the popularity of one dish is affected by the alternatives offered; you will sell more fish if the alternative is tripe, but less if it is beef! A picture of your customers' preferences and patterns of eating will emerge.

Bookings

If you take advance bookings this will indicate to some extent how busy you can expect to be on each day.

Events

The day of the week, special events in the town, market days, early closing days, bank holidays and so forth will all affect the volume of business and hence the food you must order.

Trends

Over a period, the weather, fashions and fads, and perhaps the changing profile of your customers could affect your forecast, so check it regularly to make sure that the same proportion of people are still having two or three courses, that certain items are still popular, and that, in short, you are in tune with your customers' tastes.

With a complete volume forecast you can finally plan your buying, using the number of each item, the portion sizes and the budgeted food costs to give you the quantities and prices of each item in the recipes you tested.

Buying the food

So far you have been treating food in theory. Now you must turn it into a reality and how well you do so will depend to a very large extent on how successfully you buy your raw materials. Your suppliers will be your lifeline so it is worth spending a great deal of time finding the right ones.

There are three main types of supplier — market traders, wholesalers, and cash and carry stores — and you will probably use all three for different items.

The main wholesale markets are the cheapest and often the best source of fresh foods: meat, fish and vegetables. They provide the best choice, you can see exactly what you are buying, take advantage of seasonal specialities or a glut which pulls down prices.

The main markets are also the most inconvenient way of buying. You will normally have to go in person with suitable transport to buy direct, often at highly unsociable hours of the morning to get a good choice! Buying on the market also calls for a skilled eye, especially with meat, and you may find that you have to buy a larger quantity than you can use. Finally, you may well have to pay by cash or cheque rather than on account.

Using a wholesaler overcomes several of the disadvantages of buying direct from market. Goods will be delivered, smaller quantities are available, some preparation — butchery for example — is often possible and credit accounts are quite common, once the trader knows you are creditworthy.

In return for these advantages you will pay more: most wholesale prices are about 25 per cent less than retail prices but still 10 to 20 per cent above wholesale market rates. There may also be less choice offered.

It is essential to use wholesalers you can depend on for both quality and delivery. Quality is most important for fresh produce which can vary so much. With grocery items and branded products quality will vary far less so price and delivery convenience become paramount. Hedge your bets by using more than one and bargain with them for discounts.

Wholesalers can provide everything you need but you may wish to use a local cash and carry for some items — those you use less frequently or which are very competitively priced. Again, you will need to go in person with transport but the hours of opening are far more convenient than the markets and it does help to keep up to date with new product lines. It can also be quicker to use the cash and carry than wait for a delivery when you run out of something vital, as every restaurant does, from time to time!

Whatever you buy, from whatever supplier, it is worth negotiating on price. A small discount soon adds up with the volumes involved in catering and while most discounts will depend on the quantity you buy or the value of your custom over a period, a keen bargaining sense can cut your costs significantly.

Taking deliveries

All deliveries must be checked very carefully before they are signed for. The right quality must be supplied, specially for fresh food. If the meat has too much fat or bone, refuse it or bargain on the price. If the pre-portioned steaks are too big — or small — consider carefully the effect on your food cost and customers if you accept. If the fish has too much ice in the box, your food cost will rise accordingly. If the eggs are the wrong size your omelettes will be too small or your quiches too thin.

Suppliers are not honour bound to look after your best interests. You must guard those yourself, constantly. It is not unheard of for hams to be injected with water, for ice to be added to frozen foods, for excess packing to be included in the food weight docket; these and many more tricks could make the difference between profit and loss.

On dry goods, cans, grocery items and frozen foods, quality checks depend more on the state of the packs. Tins must be free from rust, corrosion, uneven shapes from gases being produced inside, leaks and so forth. They should be labelled clearly; mistakes happen more often with catering packs than domestic and it is infuriating to open a 5-lb tin of peas to find it contains beans which are not on your menu!

Dry foods must be clean, free from contamination, in undamaged packs where appropriate. Check for broken bottles in a bulk pack or damaged containers and ask for a credit note or replacement on anything which you are not happy with.

After quality, the quantities must be checked just as carefully. The delivery note should be checked against your original order so that you can be sure that your stock level is as you planned. Then the delivery note must be checked against the actual item to detect any mistaken short supply or pilferage. Finally, your order and delivery note must be married up with the supplier's invoice before you pay it.

This all sounds time-consuming and suspicious but it is necessary. As you come to trust your suppliers you may feel you can relax your checks but don't get over-confident because it could become expensive! Sadly, the catering industry is prone to pilfering and only constant checks will make sure you do not suffer from it.

Keeping stock

How much of each item to order will depend on your volume forecasts of sales and on the stock levels you need. Overstocking is expensive because it ties up working capital and space. There is also the risk of spoilage or deterioration from over-long storage of many items, even canned and dry foods.

A good starting point is to stock up for one week's supply of dry goods and two days' supply of perishable goods, if you are certain of frequent deliveries. Where deliveries are a problem you may have to carry more dry stocks and augment fresh supplies of perishable items with carefully chosen frozen or convenience stocks.

Minimum ordering quantities may also increase the practical minimum stock level, as might trade discounts.

Once food is in stock, it should be used in date order, even those items which have a long shelf life. For most restaurants, first in first out (FIFO) is a good maxim.

You may not feel that any stock records are necessary if your restaurant is small with a limited number of items, but as a restaurant becomes larger, a simple stock record system can save time. It need be no more than a note book in which is recorded each item taken out of stock each day: the issues. Once a week or once a month, the stock is checked and the delivery notes from suppliers totalled for each item.

Stock last month + Deliveries − Issues = Stock on shelves

This simple check gives you the amount of each item that you have issued, so that you can find the food cost for the month or week. It also gives you a basic reordering list. Finally, it will check whether there is any pilfering, an important point if you have staff or if you have not been able to check all the deliveries for any reason.

If there are any discrepancies — if stock levels are lower than they should be or if the food cost is too high — then they must be investigated. Pilfering, wastage and short delivery are the most common causes.

The physical planning and conditions of the storage area or stock room are also important in stock control and are covered in the next chapter.

Drink

All of the points made above apply to drink just as much as to food. Indeed, stock control and checks are, if anything, more important for wine and spirits because of the high cost per item and the ease with which these can be smuggled out — inside or outside the offender! If anyone other than immediate family has access to the premises, a locked wine store is vital.

There should also be a good system for checking the issues of drinks, and a good stocktake. There are standard measuring sticks to use for part-full bottles of spirits which show exactly how many 'nips' are left for an accurate stocktake. The normal basis for these is 32 nips of spirit per bottle, 14 measures of sherry and vermouth and six glasses of wine (although this can vary more since no legal measure is specified for wine as it is for spirits or beers).

Preparing the food

A good catering kitchen is really a production line with the equipment and the raw materials assembled in the right places for fast action when service begins. Most of the preparation, therefore, is done in advance, as much as possible without affecting the quality of the finished meal.

Some foods can be prepared and even cooked well in advance, and kept hot until served without spoiling the quality: soups, stews and casseroles are obvious examples. Keeping food hot, however, can be dangerous unless it is kept hot enough to destroy any bacteria. And such temperatures can spoil the colour and flavour of many foods, particularly delicate sauces and vegetables, so careful planning is needed on the best order for preparing each item in advance.

Other foods are best prepared then cooled and recooked or 'finished' for final service. These might include a stock of basic sauces which are served over meat, pasta, fish or vegetables — bolognese, cream and cheese sauces and curries. A large batch sufficient for one or two days can be cooked in advance, cooled rapidly, and kept in the fridge to be drawn off in small batches or single portions as the items are ordered.

For other dishes, some advance preparation is possible but not advance cooking. Fish can be prepared ready for breadcrumbing or battering, or stuffed with prawns and rolled ready to poach at the last minute. Chicken breasts can be boned, stuffed with garlic butter and rolled ready for deep frying as chicken kiev when ordered. Meat can be trimmed, cut to size, seasoned and stored in the fridge until grilled items are called for.

Garnishes can be prepared in advance — chopped onions, parsley, tomatoes, apple sauce, stuffings, whipped cream and so forth can all be ready in the fridge for use as soon as service begins.

Vegetables are far better cooked at the last minute and used immediately but this is not always practical, especially with potatoes and vegetables which are more elaborately prepared. In this case, smaller batches can be cooked throughout service or part cooked and kept cold until the final cooking and finishing is done. Chips, for example, are cut and blanched, fried gently until soft but not coloured. When needed, they are coloured in hotter fat. Spinach is excellent dipped in boiling water for a second then plunged under cold water and kept until it is needed to be finished with hot butter or cream.

Of course, if you are using a high proportion of convenience vegetables freshness will be less of a problem, but even convenience vegetables should not be cooked too far in advance and kept hot.

The day's preparation in a restaurant will normally begin several hours ahead of service time in order for all this advance preparation — or *mise en place* — to be completed. Deliveries are usually made in the morning for preparations later in the day so that food is as fresh as possible.

Unless all the advance work is complete and stored in the right place, close to the point of final cooking and service, it will be impossible to prepare the orders quickly enough. Even in a restaurant where customers expect to take two hours to dine, they will not happily wait too long for their meal.

If you have any doubts about the importance of being well organised, spend an hour or two in a restaurant behind the scenes during service. There is no time to spare to run to the stores to get more stocks up, or to make more of a sauce or a pudding because the reserves have been used. Instead, a customer will have to be told that his choice is 'off'. It really is battle stations during service.

For this reason, it is wise to have a rest and something to eat as near as possible to service. At least ten minutes' break, sitting down and relaxing before the onslaught will save tempers later.

During service each person in the kitchen should have a clear job, according to your own pattern of work. In large restaurants it is normal to have different 'corners' in the kitchen for each separate section of the menu — cold starters, hot starters, meat, fish, vegetables, sauces, pastry and desserts. Each corner prepares its own part of a single order and the chef assembles the order at the hotplate.

This classical kitchen organisation suits only large restaurants with a complex menu. For simpler places, with perhaps only two or three people cooking, each person might take one section of the menu or one type of cooking — one on the grills, one on the deep frying and sauced dishes, one on starters and sweets.

The best division of labour will depend on your menu and on your kitchen layout because it is important to avoid too much cross traffic as people work around each other. Chapter 12 covers this in more detail.

Finally, once the main serving period is over, the kitchen must be cleared, cleaned, and preparation for the next service begun. The cleaning routine is vital, so is the disposal of waste food, especially if it has been kept hot.

The final task of the service is to check the control side of the business — the service dockets, the cash and the bills. Count the money, bag it up for the bank and prepare the cash float for the next service. Then you are ready to begin again!

Chapter 10

Kitchen Equipment

Often you will have inherited the basic kitchen equipment when you buy the restaurant and shortage of immediate funds will mean that you have to make do with it. In this case the purchase price will have included a substantial sum for 'fixtures and fittings' so it helps to know what you will need when you are evaluating the true worth of equipment during any negotiations. Having to buy the latest computerised crêpe-maker is all very well if you have a pancake house in mind; if not it is a waste of your money.

Most catering equipment is simply a larger, more robust and more practical version of domestic equipment. It is vital that any item you buy or inherit will stand up to the treatment it will get and be reliable because a breakdown will paralyse your operation.

These are the main points you should consider in choosing equipment:

- Overall quality, British standards, gas or electricity board regulations
- Fuel type and economy
- Capacity: total and convenience of handling
- Size, inside and out
- Mobility
- Compatibility with other items
- Modular, ie interchangeable with other items
- Ergonomic design: height, ease of reaching etc
- Ease of use, simplicity
- Adjustability: speeds, temperatures etc
- Flexibility: wide number of uses
- Ease of cleaning
- Maintenance: spares, servicing
- Price: initial, depreciation, running costs, insurance
- Availability: local suppliers, UK or foreign

Materials

Stainless steel is the most common material used. Its hard-wearing qualities and ease of cleaning make it an excellent material for all surfaces in a catering kitchen and for many appliances and smaller items. On larger items of equipment, stainless steel is definitely the first choice.

It is more expensive than some other materials but substituting aluminium for stainless steel pans, for example, can be false economy.

Traditionally, catering cooking utensils are made from copper lined with tin but the expense of relining with tin as it wears out and the difficulty of keeping copper clean have caused a move towards stainless steel or enamel-coated iron.

Major items

Ranges
The catering term for the modern domestic hob — the range — has four, six or eight cooking 'rings' or a solid top which normally is hotter in the centre and cooler near the outside, allowing an instant change of cooking temperature simply by moving the pan. Ranges may also have griddle plates for direct and shallow frying which are very useful because they eliminate the need for frying pans.

They are available in gas or electric models, and the average size is about 3 ft square.

Ovens
These may be under ranges — like a larger domestic cooker — or separated into banks of ovens. The average capacity of a general oven is 4 to 5 cubic feet. Smaller, shallower ovens are designed specifically for pastry and bread cooking but unless this is to be a speciality of the restaurant, the more normal general oven should suffice.

Convection ovens
A fan in the oven circulates the hot air, cutting cooking times by 30 to 40 per cent. They are useful for roasting, baking and reheating or cooking from frozen.

Microwave ovens
Increasingly popular in the home, these ovens still have limited catering use. The main drawback is that only small quantities can be cooked at one time and for maximum efficiency the food must be of uniform consistency and shape and relatively thin. The

addition of forced convection of hot air plus radiant heat for browning food has extended their usefulness but their prime use remains for reheating frozen food rapidly, for cooking the occasional item during off-peak periods or for a very specific function, such as melting cheese on burgers cooked by another method. Basically, the smaller the restaurant and the simpler the catering the more useful a microwave oven will be. Larger catering models are available and these are more efficient and more durable than domestic models and worth the extra expense if you decide to have one.

Deep fryers

A good, efficient deep fryer is an important item in almost every catering kitchen, available free standing or for mounting in a range, gas or electrically fuelled and in various sizes. The fryer should hold at least 4 to 6 inches of fat or oil and heat it to 150° to 200°C. The heating source must be powerful enough to give a fast recovery time because the fryer will have heavy use during service and most deep-fried food is cooked to order so a slow fryer will delay service.

There should be a good thermostat to control the fat temperature and avoid burning. A cool zone will collect food particles from the fat which is an expensive item, prolonging its life and making filtration of the fat easier, which also prolongs its life.

Most fryers will take 20 to 30 minutes to heat up from cold and a few minutes to regain the set temperature.

The size of fryers varies from 3 ft square to 3 × 1ft. An average-sized unit will take 40 to 60lb of chips an hour. A fryer should hold one and a half times as much food as fat, so if a fryer needs 10lb of fat it should hold 15 to 20lb of food at one time.

The capacity of fryer needed will depend on the type of restaurant and should be calculated on the quantity of chips, fried fish, and other items needed each hour.

Pressurised fryers with sealed lids can cut frying time by up to 50 per cent, saving on fuel as well.

Unless the menu is limited choice, it will be worth having two smaller fryers side by side rather than one large. This allows different operating temperatures for larger and smaller pieces of food. It also allows one fryer to be switched off during slack times, to save on fuel.

Grills

Grills operate just as domestic versions do — the main variation is in the size and robustness. Grills may heat from above (salamanders) or from below. Charcoal grills are a specialised piece of equipment.

Drip pans and grease troughs are important features to ease cleaning.

For toast, it is well worth buying a toaster rather than using the main grill. Choose one in which the separate compartments can be operated independently, for fuel economy.

Steamers

Steam cookers are usually found only in larger restaurants and industrial kitchens but they are very good for cooking vegetables because steam cooking retains the colour, texture and nutrients of food far better than boiling. Steamers are best used to batch cook, say, every 15 or 20 minutes during service. The smaller models will be cabinet-style about 12×20 inches and work under relatively low pressure of 15 psi. This size will take two or three shelves or pans.

Hot cupboards and bain maries

Holding units in the form of heated cupboards are used to store cooked food, plates, serving dishes etc for relatively short periods between cooking and service. Normal working temperatures are 75°–90°C. All food deteriorates in flavour, appearance and nutritional value when stored hot so the periods in the hot cupboard should be as short as possible. Foods such as roast potatoes, cooked pies and casseroles will keep well.

A hot cupboard 4ft wide will hold about 300 plates with sliding doors one or two sides.

A bain marie is a holding unit for foods in the form of a well or trough heated from underneath by steam, water or dry heat. Several containers of hot food sit in the well and food can be served directly from them. They are familiar equipment on self-service counters. Peas, baked beans, sauces, even some fried foods are held in these units but ideally they should be used for 'wet' food rather than grilled or fried food which should be served crisp, straight from cooking.

In choosing a bain marie, it is important to check that it will hold the containers you have, both for surface area and depth.

Normally a bain marie is 2 to 3ft from front to back and 2 to 8ft wide.

Cold storage

This covers both refrigeration and deep freeze. Total capacity of cold storage will very much depend on the menu and the amount of frozen material in use, but as a rough rule of thumb, allow between 0.25 and 0.5 cubic feet of cold storage per meal served per day.

A small restaurant may well need only one large, general fridge as close to the cooking areas as possible. Reach-in fridges are available up to about 20 cubic feet.

Larger restaurants will need more fridge space and this should be located in the main stores area, in the cooking area, and in the servery/larder/dessert service areas.

Walk-in fridges are often most practical in the main storage area. These are built on site from prefabricated panels and range in size from 50 to 100 cubic feet. Make sure that the internal shelving layout allows for maximum use of space.

Cool storage should be at $1°$ to $4°C$ for meat and fish and a little higher for dairy products.

Deep freezes operate at $-4°F$ and these, too can be chest, upright or walk in, depending on the capacity needed.

Wine storage
Wine should be stored in a dark, secure, vibration-free area which can be locked and made safe from intruders.

Red wine should be stored at $14°$ to $16°C$ and white wine at $10°$ to $12°C$. In practice, it is simplest to store both wines in the same room with white wines in the lower racks.

The wine bins can be sized to take one bottle each or a crate of each wine type, depending on the size of the stock.

General storage
General stores for dry goods should be light, dry, airy and cool ($10°$ to $21°C$). All food should be 8 inches above the ground during storage. The room should be protected against flies by gauze at the windows and against mice and rats by metal plates at the foot of external doors. Floors should be solid, free from holes and cracks.

Shelving or racks should be adjustable and designed to take heavy loads — one pack of catering sized tins will weigh over 100lb. The heaviest items should be on the lower shelves. Loose bulk items such as flour and sugar can be stored in metal or plastic bins with hinged lids which fit securely and even with wheels for easy movement.

Fresh vegetables should be stored in a cool but frost-free area which is not too dry and which has a good circulation of air both in the storage area and through the pallets or open racks in which the vegetables are stored.

Hot drinks equipment

Apart from the normal hot water supplies, restaurants need an immediate supply of boiling water for tea and coffee. The smallest boilers are electric. They produce 50, 100 or 150 pints an hour and work from a normal 13 amp socket. They are very compact but too small for anything except a snack bar which needs 3 to 10 pints of water at a time and can wait 5 to 15 minutes while the next water reheats.

Larger instantaneous boilers are gas or electric and usually stand on the floor under a cafe set or 'still' (named after the best-known supplier). Boiler capacity is usually quoted in cups or gallons per hour — and there are 18 cups to the gallon. Capacity should be chosen to cope with the busiest periods or customers will be waiting for their hot drinks which causes irritation and reduces the number of covers which can be served.

The cafe set normally consists of a coffee-making filter and steam-jacketed urns for storing the coffee and hot milk and a boiling water faucet (tap) and a steam faucet for the rapid heating of individual cups or small jugs of liquid. Larger models will also have racks for cups, saucers and service pots and jugs.

For high quality filter coffee there are various smaller machines such as Cona and individual filter jugs for presentation direct to the table. Various suppliers also make individual cup coffee filters which are thrown away after use.

Wash-up

Deep sinks big enough for dirty pots and ample hot water supplies are the basic equipment, together with good, large drainage racks and storage for clean dishes — trolleys are ideal. Double sinks allow separate washing and rinsing which minimises drying-up and allows for economical use of hot water. Cutlery racks which fit direct into work stations in the restaurant save time.

Dish-washing machines are a luxury but can pay for themselves if they save a member of staff, and washing up can be a full-time job for most restaurants.

Dishwashers vary from the smallest models, similar to domestic machines, up to large tunnel versions with conveyor belts to carry racks through. The smallest machines can cope with 125 to 200 items an hour (allow five items per meal). Larger models will take 500 plates (or 100 meals) an hour.

Dishwashers are heavy users of hot water and detergents, so good thermostats are essential and a water softener will cut detergent and rinse-aid costs.

Glass washing machines are good value especially if used under the bar which saves transporting glasses to and from the kitchen and may allow for a lower stock level as a result.

The simplest glass washers are rotating brushes fed with washing solution on to which glasses are pushed and held manually. Up to 1000 glasses an hour can be washed by automatic machines, fed on to racks.

Smaller equipment

Mixers

These are good labour savers especially with the large quantities involved in catering. They are essential for bread making, pastry work and helpful in a wide range of basic preparatory work including beating, blending, chopping, slicing, mincing etc.

For smaller restaurants an all-purpose counter-mounted mixer with a good selection of attachments is the best solution — a heavy-duty version of the larger domestic food processor. Capacities start at about 5 pints.

Work-top mixers start at about 12 pints capacity, and go up to 15 gallons. For the really large operation pedestal or floor-mounted models range from 6 to 60 gallons!

First priority is to choose a heavy-duty motor, preferably with variable speed control and an automatic timer. It should be easy to move about the kitchen. Attachments include oil droppers for making mayonnaise etc, pouring chutes, strainer, colander, cutter, shredder, chipper, bread crumber, grater and receiving trays.

Slicers

These are hand or electric, manual or fully automatic and vary in capacity from 1 to 50 slices a minute. If you need a slicer, choose one with variable speeds to allow for the different consistency of foods; slow speeds are best for hot or crumbly food while firm foods such as cold meats will take a fast speed. Slice thickness can vary from one-tenth to three-quarters of an inch.

Overall capacity is determined by the radius of the blade — 10 to 12 inches is an average size. Food is gravity fed on to the blade for easiest operation. The blade should be good quality steel for ease of sharpening and durability.

Peelers

Vegetable preparation is a time-consuming and tedious part of catering, which is why convenience vegetables are so widely used but there is still a great demand for freshly prepared vegetables so a peeler or veg prep aid is high on most caterers' lists of priority equipment.

Potato peelers are the most common but there are machines which will cope with a wider range, even irregular items such as parsnips and difficult ones like onions and soft fruits.

Smaller models are bench mounted and take 7lb of food at a time, up to 56lb. Capacity is measured also in output per hour — from 170 to 1320lb.

Whether bench or floor mounted, fixed or mobile, it is important that the machine discharges at a sensible place and height to be received in the proper place. Left- and right-hand operation is allowed for.

Most machines need a water inlet and a 2-inch waste outlet, and an electricity supply if automatic.

Some machines will chip, grate, scallop, dice and julienne — coping with, for example, 650lb of chips an hour, but these are expensive and will probably pay for themselves only in larger establishments.

In most cases, machine-prepared vegetables will need some final finishing by hand.

Small utensils

Knives are the single most important group of hand utensils. They must be top quality and there must be a good selection to cope with the various cutting jobs in the kitchen. Do not economise on knives because poor, blunt knives cause many accidents.

Pans must vary in size from the smallest for making small batches of sauces etc to the largest to cook bulk soups and vegetables.

Strainers for large volumes are best mounted on stands for ease of use. Conical shaped strainers (moulis) strain faster than rounded shapes.

Chopping boards must be very hard and easy to clean.

Small utensils are best stored in open racks under work surfaces or, for hand tools, hooked on to bars above or to the rear of work areas for quick and easy access. Knife blocks or magnetic holders mounted on walls are excellent.

Checklist for small utensils

- Cutting boards
- Mixing bowls
- Colanders
- Strainers
- Knives: vegetable, fileting, paring, chopping, cleaver, butchery, general large.
- Baking trays
- Dredgers
- Ladles
- Measures
- Spoons, paddles, stirrers
- Pans: boiling, frying
- Roasting and pie tins
- Scoops
- Scales
- Spoons
- Hooks
- Whips
- Beaters
- Cutters
- Rolling pins
- Piping bags
- Sieves
- Slicers
- Can-opener, heavy duty
- Moulds
- Bottle-opener
- Timers
- Trays
- Cutlery containers
- Toaster
- Kettles

Work flow

In catering a logical and systematic layout for equipment is vital if food is to be cooked on time with the minimum of wasted effort and without accidents. People will be rushing with hot and dangerous things so the work area must be planned to minimise cross traffic.

The simplest way to plan the kitchen is to list in order the stages the food passes through and to try and keep it flowing in one direction from delivery to storage to preparation to cooking to service and back to wash-up and waste disposal.

In practice such a simple solution is seldom possible. The physical characteristic of the premises will demand that the kitchen is as far as possible away from the stores, with tedious extra carrying. Or the only delivery access will involve crossing the paths of hurried waiting staff. Even with these difficulties, it should be possible to plan a flow chart which cuts down on cross traffic. To do this, draw out a rough sketch of the typical movements between, say stores, fridge and cooking equipment. For the service staff plan servery equipment, wash-up and collection points in a logical sequence so staff are not back-tracking and crossing each other's path.

Kitchen layouts are either wall based or island based. With wall layouts equipment is on the wall and work tables in the centre. For smaller kitchens this is probably the best layout. It is also cheaper for supplying water and main services.

Island layouts reverse the position, with groups of heavy cooking equipment in the centre and the work tables surrounding it. This allows easier access to the ranges etc for more cooks at a time in a larger kitchen.

As mentioned in Chapter 9 the classical arrangement for a kitchen is to allocate one area or 'corner' for each main food preparation and cooking function: larder work, fish, sauces, grills, frying, desserts etc. Even in a small kitchen it is a good idea to arrange specific areas for the main preparation areas. Equipment can be grouped accordingly and during service, activity will concentrate on these centres rather than everyone getting in each other's way.

Kitchens walls and floors

Restaurant kitchens soon become very dirty and greasy because of heavy usage and easy-to-clean surfaces in the kitchen are crucial, as well as being a legal requirement. Floors are best if tiled or of screed. Low noise is also helpful. Ideally floors should be laid with a 1 in 120 slope down to drains for easy sluicing down. Where walls and floors join there should be a curved coving to prevent dirt collecting, cracks appearing and insects nesting.

Walls around stoves are best lined with stainless steel or enamel-coated steel, or tiled if possible. Other walls must be hard enough to take frequent knocks as well as being easy to clean. Gloss paint on cement is an economical solution.

Chapter 11

Restaurant Equipment

Equipping the restaurant or dining room can be great fun because the design and decor will reflect your hopes and plans for the business and will imprint your personality on it.

On the other hand, you may well be short of finance to create the scheme you would like. You may have to make do with what is already supplied with the lease and with what is available at low cost. To have a restaurant professionally designed and fitted is very expensive indeed and usually beyond the scope of beginners.

Do-it-yourself is obviously cheaper but do make sure you have sufficient skill and imagination. It may be worth getting some preliminary advice from an expert interior designer to set the broad outlines for you to carry out.

The main need is to have overall harmony or a theme so that your furnishings, decor and style of catering are in sympathy. The main aim is to create a room which allows your food to be served attractively and cleanly; is comfortable, attractive and safe for both guests and staff; looks right.

From this it is clear that the restaurant must be a functional and efficient work place as well as being comfortable and attractive to customers.

The basic framework

Walls
Walls play a great part in the overall atmosphere. Natural materials such as exposed brick or wood panelling are very attractive, durable and easy to maintain. They can also be expensive to begin with. Tiles, mirrors plastics and glass can be used in some areas for contrast and practicality.

Plaster is reasonably economical, especially if it is given a textured or spray paint finish but if there is any damp it will show through. Plaster is also damaged relatively easily by knocks.

Painted finishes can be cold and harsh and should be softened by good lighting, curtains and pictures.

Wallpaper can be very attractive and relatively cheap but it is difficult to clean and will need regular replacing. A compromise is to use panelling or an expensive covering half way up the wall and paper above where it will be less easily damaged and dirtied. Use coated, wipeable papers.

Fabric tacked on to a framework of battens can be very pleasing, giving a soft, luxurious atmosphere. It is dearer than paper and equally difficult to clean although it can be spray treated to repel dirt.

Ceilings

Often restaurant ceilings are false or suspended to lower the height of an uncomfortably high room and to hide various ducting and service pipes.

Make sure that any false ceiling is easy to clean and is not a dust trap — open trellis or wood slats, for example, will soon gather dust. Ideally, a false ceiling should have no joints but be made of plaster boards or a stretched membrane. If it is jointed, as with wood panels or acoustic material or tongued and grooved strips, it is possible to make a special feature of inset lights or the occasionally varied panel.

Floors

The flooring has a great influence on comfort, noise, warmth, safety and running costs. It must be hard-wearing and easy to clean, comfortable for the staff who are on their feet all day and create the right atmosphere for customers.

Often the best solution is to have a variety of floor covering in different areas.

Rubber or PVC sheet, or plastic or vinyl tiles are practical for entrances and cloakrooms and service areas of up-market restaurants, and also for seating areas in simpler restaurants or snack bars. Such materials are easy to clean and relatively cheap but they can be marked by cigarettes and they will scuff, scratch and show wear. They are also rather functional.

Natural materials such as stone or quarry tiles, mozaics and ceramic tiles are all very attractive and hard-wearing. They can be cold and noisy, and expensive in the short term, although their durability makes them a good long-term investment.

Wood — boards, blocks or parquet — is highly decorative and gives a comfortable, warm atmosphere. It is relatively soft and will be damaged by heavy traffic. It also needs regular polishing and sealing.

Carpet is luxurious, warm and good for reducing noise. It can be bought in a wide range of colours, patterns and quality depending closely on the price. The higher the price, the longer the carpet will last and the more it will resist soiling, burning from cigarettes and wear.

Close, short pile is best as this resists wear better and is less of a 'drag' on staff feet. Carpet tiles give great flexibility as they can be moved from high to low traffic areas. In the main restaurant seating area, a medium contract grade carpet should suffice. On stairs and entrances high contract grade should be used.

Lighting

Clever lighting creates a good atmosphere more than almost any other single design factor. The right lighting will create the right mood, give texture and colour and contrast to the room and even help to disguise the shortcomings of the premises such as over-high ceilings or a badly proportioned shape.

The lighting must also be practical. Customers must be able to read the menu — not always easy by candlelight — and everyone wants to see what they are eating, however romantic they may be feeling. Staff must be able to see properly and adjust easily from the restaurant to the kitchen lighting levels, but customers should be screened from the brighter kitchen lights.

Ideally the lighting should vary with a good down light on to each table, and lower levels in the surrounding parts. Stairs, exits, and staff routes must have good light. Generally, the faster the service the higher the lighting levels.

Where there is daylight, it should be used as a good natural part of the lighting but the sun can cause glare and annoyance to customers, as can light from overstrong spotlights, glossy surfaces, mirrors and metals, so lights should be carefully positioned.

Track lighting, recessed spotlights, downlighters and dimmer switches all give great lighting flexibility, allowing an easy change of mood from one period of service to another or as the evening draws on. Candles are still very popular in many restaurants and specially designed spring-loaded catering lamps are available. Electric table lamps can cause problems with trailing wires and also take up too much space on the table, so they should be chosen with care.

Lighting fitments should be easy to clean and easy to change. Obviously they must be safe and the Electricity Board will advise on this and on correct lighting levels.

Lights can give off considerable heat but Philips has introduced a new 'SL' bulb which is said to use one-quarter the electricity of normal bulbs, last considerably longer, and produce far less waste heat. Many hotels and restaurants are switching over to the new bulbs because of these advantages but they cannot be used with dimmer switches.

A focal point

With the basic framework complete, the restaurant should be given a focal point which fits its overall image. However simple or inexpensive the menu, some photographs, pictures, plant displays, or sculpture should be included.

Antiques make a good feature and plaster cast sculptures are available at reasonable cost. Local artists and craftsmen will often provide their work at little or no cost in return for the display facilities a restaurant can provide and a very simple sales service on their behalf.

A display featuring local characters or local history is always of interest. Illustrations and photographs of the town as it was or of local attractions all add character and interest.

Ingenuity and imagination in this area can overcome the constraints of limited funds for decor to begin with. Colour used with flair in a co-ordinated way will create considerable style at little cost and give you a good basis for the furnishing and equipment which are essential and on which it is less easy to cut corners.

Restaurant furniture

Restaurant furniture is available in every style you might imagine. There are even specialists in supplying complete antique furnishing schemes for restaurants. But whether the choice is antique or modern, the essential point is strength. Restaurant furniture takes far more wear and tear than domestic furniture so check all joints, materials and coverings carefully.

Tables
The height should be 26 to 30 inches, depending on the degree of comfort. Lower tables will speed departure. The normal allowance is 2 feet of edge per person and the minimum size for a square table is 2 feet square.

Four-legged tables are cheaper than pedestals which are more flexible and comfortable. Leg levellers are a good point if you are doubtful about your floor levels.

There should be a range of tables from two to six cover sizes to allow for the optimum use of available seats whatever the size of group.

Round tables are more friendly than square but less economical on the use of space and less easy to link up if larger groups arrive.

Fixed tables and banquette seating have advantages of privacy and space economy but are also less flexible (see Chapter 6).

Table surfaces should be heat- and grease-resistant and easy to wipe clean, if no table-cloths are used. If place mats or table mats are to be used the table top material should be in sympathy with the design chosen.

Table legs can be all wood, metal or a combination, and topped with plastic, glass, wood or metal.

Chairs

Chairs must be the right height for the table: 18 inches to the top of the seat for a 30-inch high table and 17 inches high for a 29-inch table.

The width must allow the chair to be tucked under the table without hitting the legs. Armchairs are normally used only in expensive restaurants — partly because they are themselves expensive and partly because they take up considerably more space.

The back must give good lumbar support and be free of uncomfortable ridges. Where the back joins the legs there must be a very strong joint, reinforced with a spreader below the seat between the legs, plus good leg bracings.

Most restaurants will need to stack chairs from time to time, without them rubbing or catching on each other.

Upholstered chairs are also used only for more expensive restaurants. The cover should be very durable, easy to clean and stain resistant. The upholstery is normally foam 3 to 4 inches thick or the more expensive but very comfortable sprung seat.

Hardwood frames are the best for wooden chairs. The frame must be well sanded and sealed to avoid splinters and splits. Generally, wood is the most expensive material to use.

Plastic chairs are usually made of rigid urethene or impact resistant polystyrene, which is reasonably economical and available in a wide choice of colours.

Metal chairs, usually chrome or baked enamel on steel or wrought iron, are strong and durable so long as the welding is sound. They can be heavy and cold and hard to sit on for too long unless the seat is cushioned or made of a softer material.

Work stations

These are the waiting staff's sideboards, used for storing spare cutlery, china, accompaniments, and for some clearing of dirty dishes, although they should always be kept clear of dirties.

There should be one station for each member of the waiting staff, which means one per 8 to 16 covers, depending on the work load.

Purpose-built stations have shelves or cupboards, and drawers for cutlery, or runners which take the trays straight from the wash-up. Some even have small fridges for the storage of food items such as butter, milk and cream.

Otherwise work stations can be tailor made or improvised from suitable furniture which fits the overall decor. They should be 38 inches high and about 20 inches wide. They should be located no closer than 4 feet from customers' tables because of the noise and disturbance.

Linen

The choice of linen will depend on the style of the restaurant and the decor. Paper serviettes and place mats with a personalised design may be suitable, or cork or laminated mats with a higher quality paper serviette.

As the standard of the restaurant rises, so table-cloths become the norm, together with fabric napkins or the highest quality paper products.

Table-cloths are available in a wide range of colours, shapes, patterns and materials. The best quality remains linen, and it is still the most commonly used in top restaurants. There is a variety of grades, depending on the number of threads per inch. It remains popular, despite its expense, because it is smooth, soil resistant, holds a crease well and is available in self-patterns.

Cotton on its own will crease and soil easily but blending it with linen or nylon overcomes these drawbacks to some extent. Although it comes in good colours, these do fade.

To combine the best of both worlds, many restaurants use top quality undercloths with coloured slips which can be changed quickly and are easier to launder, thus cutting costs and adding flexibility as well.

Linen hire services for cloths, napkins and waiters' cloths are sometimes the most convenient and economical way of handling linen.

Depending on the efficiency of the laundry arrangements, you will need six sets of linen per cover — one on the table, and one in the collection room, the laundry, on the return, in the restaurant and in the linen store as reserve.

You should allow replacement at the rate of 20 per cent a year.

Menus

The menu design is very important. It must be easy to read and simple to understand, a tool which helps to sell your food by whetting appetites, in sympathy with the overall style and level of the restaurant, and flexible enough to allow unexpected price and dish changes.

The most common arrangement is a simple menu card which is easily altered by re-typing or reprinting. In simpler restaurants this card alone will suffice but in more expensive restaurants the card(s) are normally set into a more eleborate menu holder. The price of these can range from £2.50 for a simple plastic holder to £30 for a real leather, gold overprinted case.

Feature menus include parchment scrolls, chalked blackboards brought to the table on an easel, illuminated panels fully illustrated (for fast food bars and self-service counters) or even no menu at all; instead the patron recites the dishes and their compilation which can be time-consuming in all but the smallest place but is a very personal approach.

If your menu changes daily or weekly you will need some way of producing menus. Often a good typewriter is the answer, or standard printed menus into which you can handwrite the dishes of the day. Menus written in good, clear, attractive handwriting can be more than acceptable, or you may want to invest in a small copier or duplicator of some kind.

China and glass

These are expensive items simply because of the quantities needed. 'China' or tableware must be light, durable, attractive, scratch- and chip-resistant, the right shape, easy to stack, easy to replace and with strong rims which take the weight if stacked to avoid scratching the main surface. There should be a good range of sizes and shapes, with handles well jointed, lips that pour easily and safe lids.

Vitreous hotelware is the first choice for most restaurants. It is strong, light and therefore easy for staff to carry. There is a good choice of designs and it combines attractiveness with reasonable cost.

Metallised bone china is also specially designed for restaurants. It has all the advantages of vitreous hotelware plus some of the attractiveness of bone china but it is also expensive.

Bone china is, surprisingly, very strong. It looks beautifully delicate but it is very expensive.

Vitrified earthenware is strong but heavy and lacks the attractiveness of other choices.

Glazed earthenware is weak and can chip easily. It is heavy to carry and must be well glazed if it is to last. It is very pleasing to the touch.

Stoneware is good for a country style feel and for oven-to-table ware, jugs, bowls, casseroles etc. It comes in a limited range of darker colours and is heavy to carry.

Although oval plates are available, circular ones are most practical and easy to carry. Usual plate sizes are 175 mm, 230 mm and 255 mm. Cup sizes are 4, 6, 7 and 8 fluid oz.

Glasses must be available in sizes which match your needs, and in shapes and designs which fit your image. They must be as durable as possible, well designed with good strong stems and joints, easy to store and stack where possible and shaped for easy cleaning.

Cut glass — usually full lead crystal — is very expensive, even in catering ranges, but is is used by top restaurants in both traditional and modern designs.

Tempered glass is specially toughened.

Common glass sizes are:

Tumblers	8, 10, 12 fluid oz
Beer	$\frac{1}{2}$ and 1pt — with a government stamp if you are selling from the pump
Wine and spirits	5, 6, 8 fluid oz
Port, sherry	$2\frac{1}{2}$ or 3 fluid oz
Liqueurs	$1\frac{1}{4}$ fluid oz

Apart from drinks glasses you may need glass for food service including sundaes, fruit and fish cocktails and some desserts.

Metalware

This includes cutlery, serving dishes, cruets and hot drinks containers. Metal serving dishes are stronger and lighter than 'china', they heat better and if made of the right material, resist scratching and corrosion.

Copper lined with tin is expensive, needs frequent cleaning and is heavy. It loses its heat quickly and must be relined to prevent contamination of food once the tin wears thin. It is, however, a traditional catering material and is extremely attractive if properly maintained.

Aluminium is not really acceptable for the restaurant although it is used in the kitchen. It does not have an attractive appearance because it scratches so easily and looks dull.

Stainless steel is very strong and is available in matt or polished finish. It can look dullish but is reasonably economical.

Electro-plated nickel silver (EPNS) is very attractive and correspondingly more expensive. It is soft and will dent as well as tarnish. The price is determined by the thickness of the plate, as is the durability. All catering standard plate should last 20 years. EPNS is the usual metalware for expensive restaurants but its use may well call for a burnisher or considerable staff time in polishing it.

For cutlery the basic choice is between EPNS or stainless steel for the metal, with metal, wood or nylon handles. If the handle is formed separately from the blade it must be soundly joined. It is best to stay with the most common designs rather than 'new' shapes which may confuse customers — four-pronged forks are still easier to eat with although harder to clean than three pronged.

There is a wide choice of designs available. Experiment by trying out the short-listed ranges with the chosen china to ensure that teaspoons will not fall off saucers and that knives are not handle-heavy and will stay on plates when clearing is under way.

Minimise the different items used and double up on functions when possible for ease of operation — butter knives can serve as fruit knives, fish cutlery is less common than it was, some spoons will function as both soup and dessert...

For security, it is wise to have expensive cutlery badged with your name. Normal stock levels are four sets per cover.

Miscellaneous items

Flats for 'silver' service
Flats covers

Tureens
Jugs
Bowls
Teapots
Coffee pots
Sugar bowls
Cruets
Mustard and sauce containers
Ashtrays
Flower vases
Sweet, cheese and dessert trolleys
Cash desk
Coat hangers

Bar equipment

If you have space for a separate bar area it should include cold shelves for mixers and chilled beers, a small sink for washing glasses and spills disposal; optics for the dispense of spirits (or measures) and good storage space for glasses and bottles, including probably a simple wine dispense with stocks of wine for service in the near future. Accessories include cocktail-making equipment, and ingredients such as lemons, olives, peels, cream, sugar, bitters, and ice.

If cold drinks and cocktails play a large part in your menu an ice maker may be justified. Machines need a 13 amp power point, a $\frac{3}{4}$ inch plastic drain at or below ground level with a trap, and a mains water inlet solely for the machine.

For a 30-seater restaurant a machine able to produce 50lb of ice and store 30lb (12 buckets) would suffice.

A large restaurant would need a machine which could make 150lb and store 90lb (30 buckets).

Chapter 12

Daily Operation

The day starts early in a restaurant. Although it is no longer necessary for the most junior member of the kitchen team to rise before dawn to light the coal-fired cooking ranges, there is still a great deal of preparation to be done before the service starts.

A well run restaurant is based on good planning and adequate advance preparation. Without this, service will be slow and disorganised, customers will be unhappy (so will staff) and the business will suffer.

Surprisingly, the pattern of the day will not differ greatly from one restaurant to another, whatever the style and hours of service. The amount of advance work will obviously be less in a restaurant which relies heavily on convenience foods and has a very simple menu. Most advance work will be needed in the luxury restaurants offering complicated menus and gourmet food — much of which has to be cooked to order.

For each service period, there are three main periods: preparation, service and clearing away.

This pattern will apply to all restaraunts, whether they are open continuously for 12 hours a day or open in two separate sessions for lunch and dinner. A restaurant which is open continuously will be carrying out some preparation and clearing away work during the quieter service periods rather than having such clearly defined splits to the day, but the principle is the same.

Most restaurants start work anything from one to four hours before they are formally open, depending on the style of food and service.

Kitchen preparation

In a restaurant which opens for lunch at 12 or 12.30, the kitchen staff and management will be hard at work from 8 or 9 am, together, perhaps, with a cleaner to help with the heaviest tasks of cleaning. Their first duties will be to check stock levels, making sure there are sufficient supplies for the immediate needs of the day, ordering perishable items for delivery before the service, and doing a regular checking and ordering for dry goods and items with a longer life. In some cases the chef or proprietor will visit the markets to buy. Throughout the preparation period, suppliers will be delivering goods and these must be carefully checked for quality and quantity and against delivery notes.

Once ordering is complete, items needed for the coming service must be drawn out of the main stores into the kitchen or preparation area and any stock control documentation must be done. Then preparation starts in earnest with the cooking. Just how much cooking can be done in advance will depend on the style of restaurant and its menu. A menu heavily dependent on convenience foods or simple snacks and grills will need less advance cooking than a restaurant which prepares all its own items.

A gourmet restaurant will want to cook as much as possible to order because this produces the best quality — keeping food hot or reheating it does impair its texture, colour, taste and nutritional value in direct proportion to the time it is kept hot. On the other hand, a gourmet restaurant will probably be offering more complex dishes calling for many different ingredients, so much of the advance work will not be in complete cooking but in producing *mise en place* — assembling all the raw ingredients as far as possible without finally putting them all together. Typical items will be stocks, basic sauces, thickening agents, chopped herbs, onions, tomato concasse, sweated mushrooms and shallots, prepared garnishes, trimmed, boned and seasoned meats and fish, breadcrumbs, batters, coatings, all of which can be combined when a dish is ordered, while the customer is enjoying a leisurely aperitif and starter.

A restaurant catering for middle-of-the-road popular foods with a degree of home cooking will need to cook far more dishes completely in advance, in order to achieve the speed of service its customers expect. Roasts, soups and casseroles will all be completely ready for service by the start of the session.

Obviously the cooking must start with the items which take longest or are needed in order to complete a dish: stocks, stews and basic sauces which need a long, slow cooking period will be put on first, followed by roasting joints which will need several hours because of their large size and the need to cut shrinkage with slower cooking.

Once these items are under way the cooks can prepare those dishes which need more of their time and attention but have shorter cooking periods — vegetable preparation is a typical example. The sheer volume involved takes a considerable time, even with the machines outlined in Chapter 10, but once done the cooking times are usually quite short and vegetables, above all, are best cooked as late as possible.

Finally, garnishes will be prepared; meat and fish for grilling or frying (which must be cooked to order) will be trimmed and put back in the fridges; cold items will be finished and put in the fridge so that they are sufficiently cold.

As all the food is completed, ready for service, it must be kept hot in the best way: wet food, food which can be held in hot water or is in sauces which will not separate, can be kept in a bain marie. Roasted items, many vegetables and 'dry' foods can be held on a hotplate under covers or not, depending on whether the steam generated will impair them.

Once the advance cooking and preparation are complete, there is normally a break of 30 or 45 minutes for rest and meals. This is well earned and also necessary if people are to give their best during the often hectic service period when speed is needed.

After this, while the service gets into full gear, the last minute items can be prepared.

Kitchen service

Once customers have arrived, the focal point of the kitchen is the hotplate where orders arrive and are called out so that the relevant cook can prepare the dish. In a small kitchen this will be whoever is least busy — assuming there is more than one cook! In a very large kitchen, there will be separate sections, 'corners' or 'parties' for each section of the menu — meat, fish, deep fried items, sauces, vegetables, desserts. Each section will prepare its part of an order and the final checking and assembling will be done by the chef at the hotplate as he checks the dishes against the written order from the waiting staff.

This is usually a very busy and noisy time in the kitchen when good working relationships and good teamwork are vital. Much will depend on the character and personality of the chef or the head cook, who should be able to keep everything running smoothly with no bottle-necks or delays.

Clearing away
As the tempo of service slows, kitchen staff can begin clearing away and cleaning up the kitchen, with the help of the staff responsible for washing up pots and kitchen equipment.

Unsold food must be saved and stored for reuse or disposed of.

117

Equipment must be switched off as soon as possible to save fuel. General cleaning must be done. Any further paperwork must also be fitted in, as must extra ordering and menu planning.

If the restaurant continues to be open to customers, there will be the occasional order which needs work from the kitchen, but otherwise most of the time will be available for preparation work for the next main meal service.

If the restaurant closes between lunch and dinner the kitchen staff will want to be off duty as soon as possible for a well earned rest before the long evening shift. In this case, staff should be released one at a time and the first off duty should be the first back to start the evening's preparation

Preparing the restaurant

Service staff should normally be on duty three-quarters to one and a half hours before the restaurant opens, depending on how much preparation there is to be done. In simpler restaurants the service staff are often responsible for some of the food preparation as well — bringing cold items from the main fridge to the still room or larder service area, checking that the dessert service area is properly stocked, that cold starters are ready, preparing bread, assembling cold accompaniments and sauces, preparing coffee and other hot drinks.

Ideally, one or more service staff should be allocated to this preparation behind the scenes while others are responsible for checking linen, preparing the laundry for delivery, laying the tables, and for light cleaning duties such as dusting the restaurant and polishing the shiny surfaces. The main cleaning should be done by a cleaner. Menus must be written or updated and generally kept in good order. The sideboards must be well stocked with spare cutlery and china plus all the necessary accompaniments and cruets which will be needed during service.

If advance bookings are taken, service staff should be responsible for keeping the diary and allocating the reserved tables to each party.

The cash desk must also be made ready and this should be done by the proprietor or a manager. The cash float must be available — and this may entail a visit to the bank. The till roll must be zeroed and working correctly and all necessary stationery — bill books, order pads, table cards — must be ready for use with starting numbers recorded.

If there is a separate bar the barman or one of the service team must make sure it is well stocked with clean glasses brought from the wash-up and with canned and bottled items drawn from the stores. Ice buckets must be filled, slices of lemon, mint, cherries and other garnishes prepared, beer pumps cleaned, checked and refilled if necessary. Any nuts, crisps, olives or other titbits should be placed round the area and ashtrays made available.

The cloakroom should be checked for all supplies, particularly paper, soap and towels.

When the room is ready, the service staff should also have a rest period and meal or a snack, depending on your policy.

The only type of restaurant which will differ greatly from this pattern of activity is a self-service one where the emphasis will be on preparing the counter rather than laying up tables. Apart from that, many of the duties must still be carried out.

Restaurant service

As in the kitchen, the service period is the busiest and noisiest, with staff working as fast as they can — ideally!

Staff should be trained to welcome customers with a friendly greeting and perhaps an indication of a suitable table so that customers are made to feel welcome and noticed even if your style is not to have a formal 'greeter and seater'.

As soon as a person is seated there should be some immediate attention given — whether it is bringing the menu or offering bread rolls or an aperitif. The order should be taken as soon as possible, and most customers give reasonably clear signals when they are ready to order. Rapid order taking aids the flow of work into the kitchen, keeps the customer content and helps a fast turnover if this is what is needed.

As service proceeds, staff should keep a careful check on the kitchen's progress so that orders are not waiting too long for collection — often some signal such as a bell is helpful.

The focal point of the service staff is the sideboard or service station which is a staging post for picking up and putting down items and for storing all manner of smaller items needed during service.

All the usual rules of service are still valid and are appreciated by customers even in an informal restaurant — ladies served first, cold items served first, dishes put down from the left and cleared from the right, don't clear until all members of a group have finished, regular attention to the service of bread and drinks. Prompt clearing away as cleanly and easily as possible....

A good rule of thumb for service staff is 'never go into the kitchen empty handed'. Invariably there are dirty items on the sideboard and if these are left there is nowhere to put fresh food on the return journey from the kitchen.

As customers finish their meals the bills must be prepared and presented either when called for (in a gourmet restaurant) or as soon as possible (in a fast service restaurant where a quick turn-over is needed). If a cashier prepares the bills the service staff must ensure that all requisition slips are with the cashier; if they prepare their own bills they should complete them as soon as the meal is finished so that they are ready when needed.

During any lulls in service, sideboards can be restocked and tidied and a watchful eye kept on customers who might want service.

Clearing away

As customers leave, the service staff are usually kept fairly busy clearing away the tables and relaying them for another sitting. As much of this as possible is done in advance, although tables are not left laid up overnight.

Ideally, by the time lunch service is over, the restaurant should be ready for dinner, with all tables laid and sideboards restocked. This allows the evening service staff to come on duty only a short period before the restaurant opens.

After service the cash must be counted and reconciled with the bill totals, the float redone ready for the next session and the main bookkeeping work for the period completed, together with any banking.

This is particularly important if there is a change of staff in a continuous service restaurant, so that any errors can be isolated and the person responsible identified.

Staff rotas

The staff rota should reflect as closely as possible the peaks and troughs in the pattern of business and the flow of work. Catering staff are used to working flexible hours and this allows you to roster staff so that they are there only when needed. Thus in the kitchen it should not be necessary to have all the staff on duty for an entire shift. At the peaks of preparation and service a full rota is vital but during the 'shoulder' periods either side of the peak it should be possible to release staff. This saves valuable hours and may make it possible to manage with one member of staff less.

The same applies to the service staff. Rotas should be an overlapping pattern of early and late shifts, often determined by an individual's preference, giving maximum staffing at the busiest periods.

The tradition in the business is split shifts and, although the trend is to offer staff straight shifts wherever possible, this cannot always be done, especially in smaller restaurants, but often part-time staff are available to ease the load on full-timers.

Once the rota is prepared, do check regularly that staff can work accordingly and be prepared for illness or some other cause giving a last minute panic. On these occasions it is invaluable to have on call some part-time or casual staff who will step in to help out although other members of staff may be prepared to work overtime.

If the restaurant is open until late at night it may be necessary to offer transport home — either a lift in your own car or a paid taxi fare.

The daily operation of a restaurant is a constant flow of work involving attention to details and response to people. It is demanding and exhausting but it is also very fulfilling and satisfying, even if you're crawling out of the door because your feet hurt so much!

Finally, however great the temptation, do take a break when the hours permit. You, your staff and most of all, your restaurant, will benefit from even an hour spent away from the business.

Chapter 13

The Way Ahead

What next? You're running your own restaurant; it's successful and you've coped well with the teething troubles. Now, perhaps for the first time since you started, you have time to look ahead and decide what to do next. That might involve changing your style of business or developing it. You might want to expand — enlarge the restaurant or even start a second one. Or perhaps bring in a manager so that you have more time to enjoy the results of your enterprise.

It is important to consider the direction you wish to take. Often the first year or so of a new venture takes so much time and energy that you scarcely have time to think longer term; survival is all. But forward planning is important too, especially in a business like catering which is increasingly fashion-conscious.

Following fashion

Even a brief visit to London or any large metropolitan city will allow you to inspect some of the latest trends in restaurants and to try the current food fads. Not all will succeed and not all deserve to. However, there are clear trends in eating habits which should be reflected in your own menu — perhaps through gradual and gentle changes rather than a drastic overhaul. More health-conscious foods, lighter styles of cooking, more attractive presentation, more imaginative flavour combinations ... all have a place on today's menu, keeping you in touch with tomorrow's customers.

Although your present formula may be popular and successful, don't forget that your regular customers could become bored if you don't offer them something new from time to time. Keep some surprise and sparkle in your restaurant if you want to keep your regulars.

You may also find that although your restaurant is popular, it is not meeting your financial targets. The spending power may be too low or your speed of service too slow to achieve the necessary turnover. Such problems call for a rethink of the menu and service methods and this will be easier if you are aware of the long-term trends and underlying changes in people's eating habits, as well as understanding your own market and what people find attractive about your restaurant.

New technology

If you started your restaurant on a shoe string an early priority might be to improve the decor, furnishings and equipment. Again, don't spoil a successful formula but do consider carefully if the extra investment will bring extra business or make you more efficient and therefore more productive.

This is particularly important with large items of kitchen equipment. Often an older hand-me-down model performs just as well as a new, expensive one, so make sure that there really is a valid reason for splashing out.

Some new pieces of equipment do offer definite technical advances. Convection and forced-air ovens cut cooking time and allow you to improve service; deep fat fryers can pay for themselves in fat and fuel savings; microwave ovens can extend your service capabilities in certain (limited) circumstances; dishwashers and vegetable preparation equipment can be real lifesavers.

Computers are making their debut in kitchens, as elsewhere, but it will probably be some time yet before the small independent restaurateur can justify their use. Automatic metering for bulk recipes; automatic timing and temperature controls, computerised stock controls . . . these are typical applications and of more value to the largest scale industrial kitchens.

The computer will almost certainly be of value to you in administration and the front of house. A small computer could handle all the necessary bookkeeping so if you are computerate, by all means use one. If, however, you are totally new to the business, the best advice is to become fully familiar with it and a manual set of books before you think about computerising. That way you will understand your business better and choose the most suitable computer when the time is right. An electronic cash register, although expensive, can be used for sales analysis, and summarise daily totals for you under the various headings.

Looking further ahead, in America there is now a restaurant offering customers a table top VDU through which they can order their meal direct to the kitchen. A real person still delivers it but no doubt a robot will take this over in due course! Overall, the scope for technical developments is still limited. A restaurant is a personal and labour-intensive business and only the largest scale operations can really justify the investment that high technology demands, or risk the loss of the personal touch it brings.

Expansion

The most difficult decision you will probably have to face is whether or not to expand and, if you decide to do so, how to do it. The scope for expanding your existing premises is likely to be limited although it is by no means unheard of for a restaurant with nightly queues to take over the shop next door. But more often, a larger restaurant will mean a move and perhaps starting again from scratch to build up your business in its new location.

The main difficulty with expansion is that you will almost certainly have to delegate some of your own involvement and you will soon discover that no one will run the business the way you want or as well as you do! At best they will not do things as well as you wish; at worst they will be negligent or dishonest.

Bringing in a partner or relative to help is not always the solution and many partnerships fail quite soon because of personal or business disagreements.

However, if you want to expand you must resolve these problems. The first stage is to find ways of exercising your control on the things which are most important to you and the success of the business. Usually this will mean giving up day-to-day involvement in the preparation and execution of tasks and concentrating instead on supervising others to do the work. This in turn will increase your staff costs since you will have to pay someone to do what you did previously, but you are almost certainly better employed supervising the kitchen rather than peeling the potatoes!

If and when you bring in management help, hire the best you can afford with the personality to fit into your team and the way you work. Qualifications and experience will give you some guidance but you may be best advised to take on someone you like and can trust who can be trained in your methods, rather than taking the best qualified.

Most of the foregoing applies if you are expanding into one larger restaurant. Expansion by opening a second unit brings additional problems, simply because you cannot be in two places at once.

The danger here is that the character and appeal of most

private restaurants still depends very heavily on the personality and presence of the owner. Even if you remain firmly behind the scenes, your involvement will be influencing the people serving customers. Chain restaurants and group owned businesses replace this charisma with stylish decors, greater atmosphere, expensive themes and, perhaps, heavy promotional budgets. Such substitutes may well be outside your budget but you cannot afford to underestimate the great part your own presence plays in the success of your restaurant, so think and plan carefully before taking on number two.

Expansion can also drain your resources. Because you are less closely involved you will need tighter management controls to check how the business is running. You will rely more on systems, reports and the efficiency of other people. You will need meetings and a tighter organisation.

Once you move into this stage of development you are moving into the realms of the less personal restaurant and your involvement will be that of a director more than a proprietor. This may well appeal to you, and if you have a successful formula which you are convinced is worth extending, you may be thinking in terms of raising further capital, perhaps through equity sharing or a franchise offer.

At this stage the same criteria for financial planning apply as they did first time round but this time you will need to allow for finance charges and the extra staffing and management costs.

Of course, if you have reached this stage you will already have achieved success, so identify what factors made that success and don't sacrifice them in the name of expansion. Equally, be clear about what gives you satisfaction from your restaurant, whether it is the daily contact with customers, the varied tasks of preparation, cooking, buying and administration and whether you would be as happy concentrating on just one or two aspects. Above all, it's worth remembering that bigger is not always better, especially in a restaurant.

Chapter 14

A Restaurateur's Story — A Case History of Success

Doug Palmer opened his first restaurant in Basingstoke, Hampshire in 1979, achieving a long-held ambition.

Small beginnings

It cost him £3,000 then to open the doors of the 36-seater 'bistro' after six months of hard work to get it ready. His wife gave up her teaching job to help establish the restaurant but because they opened only in the evenings for the first year, Doug was able to keep on his own job as deputy director of the local sports centre.

The Palmers borrowed no money for their venture; instead they used savings and the proceeds of selling the car.

The menu at the Bistro was very simple — grills, steaks, spaghetti bolognese, chilli con carne ... all home cooked and served in the friendly, informal cottage-style restaurant. (Doug places great importance on his restaurant being attractive and in a style sympathetic to the building it occupies.)

The average spend in the early days was £3 a head, and there is no doubt that the restaurant filled a large gap in the market in Basingstoke, a fast-growing town where leisure facilities had not kept pace with the boom in housing and commerce.

From day 1 Doug employed a chef; his wife ran the front of the house and he assisted in the kitchen. 'I've always been able to cook' he says, 'but doing it in a restaurant can be vastly different — all our dishes were cooked individually to order and this calls for a different kind of skill from making something at home by following a recipe and working at your own pace.'

That first year was 'the hardest of my life — a continuous cycle of work and sleep with no time off', says Doug. He would have sold up at this stage, but the short lease on the premises meant it would have been hard to find a new occupier. In any case, the Bistro was very popular and busy most nights, so to give it up would have seemed like quitting in the face of success!

Instead of selling up Doug gave up his job which relieved a lot of the pressure. It also meant opening for lunch to fill the financial gap now that there was no other source of income.

It soon became obvious to Doug that the Bistro was not producing the money he needed to meet the overheads. The reason was simple — the prices were too cheap and as Doug says, 'It doesn't take a financial genius to work out £3 times, say, 28, which is the most you're likely to serve with a 'full' restaurant, after allowing for wasted seats.' On this basis the Palmers could not have survived for long.

Gradually they made the necessary changes. They pushed up the prices and the resulting average spend, justifying the increases with a more elaborate menu and a better standard of service, and their customers stayed loyal.

The Bistro ran for seven years until the lease expired. During those years Doug learned a great deal by practical experience, but much of his success is due to his own beliefs about restaurants and what people like.

One early mistake he made was to open with a blaze of publicity and a generous opening discount offer.

'It was a mistake,' he admits. 'The best advice I can give is to open quietly, especially if it's your first restaurant. You don't want to be packed out when your systems are untried and unpractised. Allow in your costs for three or four quiet weeks — the initial curiosity of people will carry you through so you won't be empty. Then when the first interest starts to decline you can promote the restaurant and begin to look for regular custom to build up.'

Those seven years at the Bistro gave Doug the experience and the confidence to open his second, much larger restaurant and to go on to even greater success.

From strength to strength

It took many months to find the right premises for the successor to the Bistro. Doug was looking for a much bigger place with character in the town centre and he finally found it in an older pedestrianised street at the top of the town.

The building had been a bookshop and coffee shop so planning consent was relatively straightforward. And although the building needed a lot of work, the landlord had planned improvements before reletting and agreed to carry out much of the reconstruction work to Doug's specification — developed with the help of an interior designer friend.

This time it took a year to reach opening day and Doug spent every spare minute he could on the project.

'Palmers' opened on 29 February 1984 — as quietly as possible, given that Doug had a very loyal clientele who followed him from the Bistro.

The atmosphere at Palmers is spacious, airy, light and relaxed. Natural wood floors and furniture, mirrors and plants plus neutral colours create a simple but effective restaurant which seats 50 downstairs and 50 upstairs in a room used almost entirely for private parties.

The menu is very similar to the final Bistro menu which had been developed over the years and proved so popular. 'You don't change a successful formula although we did add some new ideas,' says Doug. All the hot starters can be ordered as a main course while vegetarian and whole foods play an important part on the menu. 'Anyone in catering has to take this seriously now,' he says. All the food is home cooked; all produce is bought fresh from the markets including the meat.

The menu offers a wide choice; it is changed regularly and there is an additional, weekly changing menu as well. The more unusual dishes include:

Ham and asparagus pancakes
Kachori (Indian dumplings filled with spicy vegetables, rice and coconut)
Nut roast
Herrings in oatmeal
Local trout stuffed with lemon and thyme
Noisettes provençal

Starter prices range from 95p for homemade soup to £2.85 for Mediterranean prawns tossed in hot garlic butter. Main courses are from £3.20 for cannelloni to £6.95 for beef Wellington or sole and prawn thermidor. Fresh-cooked vegetables are 85p or 95p and all prices include VAT. Service is 'at your discretion'.

Pattern of business

Palmers is open for lunch and dinner seven days a week and there is no fixed pattern of quiet or busy days although Sunday lunch is usually the slowest . Occasionally there may be two or three quiet days in a row which is 'pretty depressing' but when Doug analyses the business on a monthly basis the total sales per month are relatively constant.

Mondays to Thursdays the main source of trade is business people visiting Basingstoke, staying in hotels and wanting to eat out both at lunch-time and in the evening. Friday lunch is often busy with office parties. At weekends the trade is purely local and Doug takes pride in the fact that his restaurant appeals to all age groups. 'By being genuinely pleased to see all our customers we manage to attract families, young people, business parties and older people. In fact the mix of customers on any one occasion is quite dramatic and this is reflected in the very wide fluctuation in customer spend.'

Average spend

The average spend is more of a range at Palmers — from £5 to £15. The menu is deliberately designed for this because of Doug's strong conviction that 'it is essential to have a full restaurant. My guiding principle has always been first to set the right prices to attract customers and then worry about the margins. After all, it's better to have 40 per cent of something than 60 per cent of nothing.'

This policy results in Palmers' customers being given good value and generous portions and because the restaurant is busy enough, it is also profitable.

Credit cards

Payments by credit cards account for almost a third of turnover — which means hefty commission payments to the card companies. This is an overhead often overlooked but it can make a big hole in profits; in the case of Palmers, credit card commissions are the fourth largest overhead, exceeded only by wages, rent and the bill for heat, light and fuel.

Doug says, 'I aim to make 10 per cent net profit but if a customer pays a £10 bill with a credit card, the card company makes 50p — the same as I do!'

Promotion

Palmers' promotion budget is about £2000 in 1985–86. Most of this is spent supporting the local charities by donating meals or wine as raffle prizes which Doug sees more as a goodwill gesture than promotion as such. He does have a small monthly advertisement in the local paper when it publishes its regular feature on

129

the 'Top of the Town' but he has not been able to assess how useful this is.

He remains convinced that the best form of promotion is word of mouth: 'Every customer who goes out of your door will do your advertising for you if they've had a good time.'

Staff and management

There is a total of 30 staff, 15 full time and the rest part time, working between nine and 30 hours a week. Some part-timers may do just a single session of washing up while full-time staff work four or four-and-a-half day weeks, each day being composed of two shifts.

The total of 30 includes a restaurant manager who was appointed six months before opening day. A qualified caterer, he and Doug share the duty sessions of restaurant manager — he works four 12-hour days and Doug works three. Initially this gave Doug more time for planning and preparation for the opening and now it gives him some time for administration and general management of the business and, hopefully, some time to relax away from it with his children and his wife who is no longer involved in the daily running of the restaurant.

Both Doug and the manager try to steer clear of the daily routine tasks in order to deal with the day-to-day problems, meet customers and supervise the general running. In practice, they both get involved in everything, from watering the plants to mending the roof!

The head chef, a woman, has complete control of the kitchen: she is salaried and works as necessary, depending to some extent on the private function bookings. Two assistant chefs are normally responsible for the main à la carte cooking, working in split shifts four days a week.

The normal staffing level for each day is:

Kitchen	head chef
	2 assistant chefs
	washer-up
Restaurant	1 restaurant manager
	3 waiting staff
	1 bar person
Administration	1 assistant manager(ess) full time for functions, personnel
	1 accountant/bookkeeper (part time)
General	1 early morning cleaner

Doug advertises locally to find staff but says: 'It's enormously difficult getting the right people. We look for more than experience although we prefer it and it's essential in the kitchen. But we also want like-minded people who get on with our sense of humour and can be one of the team. Once they join us, people tend to stay. Staff turnover is very low —all the staff from the Bistro are still with us, but when we do need staff, it's a problem to find them.'

There is no staff uniform as such but the waiting staff must wear plain red, white or black in suitable materials and styles and kitchen staff must wear clean whites. In return, staff receive a clothing allowance which is paid as a lump sum quarterly in arrears.

Any tips are shared equally between all staff on duty and Doug leaves this entirely to the staff to organise.

Staff costs

For the first year, staff costs were 20 per cent of turnover, including Doug's own salary. He judges efficiency by the customer to staff ratio as much as by staff costs. His target is 10 customers for each member of staff on duty which is the level achieved at the Bistro and, although it was difficult to achieve in the first year of a new restaurant, the final results are only slightly below this and should improve in the second year, once staff are familiar with the systems and with working together.

Senior members of staff are on bonus system which relate to gross profits and turnover.

Gross profits

Doug's target is 50+ per cent gross profit but he accepts 50 per cent, and in his first year the final result was 51 per cent. He accepts that there is extra cost and more waste with home cooking and fresh produce but feels the higher quality is worthwhile.

Daily routine
6 am   Early morning cleaner arrives to clean and receive deliveries.

9.30 am Duty manager, administration team and kitchen staff arrive. Duty manager checks staff rotas, bookings, function groups.

	Head chef does purchase orders, stock checks.
	Assistant manager arranges menus, checks function and dining rooms.
	Kitchen staff prepare food.
11 am	Restaurant staff on duty. Set up dining room.
12 am	Service starts.
2 pm	Last orders. Tables relaid.
3.15 pm	Close. Duty manager cashes up, checks evening float.
6.30 pm	All staff on duty. Final preparations.
7 pm	Evening service starts.
10 pm	Last orders (except theatre bookings).
12 pm	Close. Duty manager cashes up.

What makes success?

Like most restaurateurs, Doug finds it hard to explain his success: 'I can't really pinpoint one thing — it's more of an intuitive feeling, a sensitivity. It really doesn't take much to please people, just a few words or a little something extra and of course, the food must be good. I do find I have to be annoyingly fussy about seemingly trivial details. I know what the standard should be and it's up to me to maintain it. If I allow anyone to fall below the standards I set, I'm dropping to their level and it happens that they are working in *my* restaurant — not the other way round!'

The future

'I'm not running the sort of restaurant which is easy to duplicate because we are not a standard package. The restaurant is run by a team of hard-working, caring individuals; and therefore it's unique.

'I'm sure that there's an opening in catering for a *good* standard product but how you achieve it, I don't know. You couldn't do it without individual attention and personalised service. The person with the responsibility must be fully involved to maintain the standards — that's what I've always found and I can't see it changing in the future.'

Appendices

Appendix 1

Further Reading

Catering

Atkinson, *Menu French* (Pergamon Press)

Bull and Hooper, *Hotel and Catering Law* (Hutchinson)

Ceserani, Lundberg and Kotschevar, *Understanding Cooking* (Edward Arnold)

DHSS 1971, *Clean Catering* (HMSO)

Escoffier, *The Complete Guide to the Act of Modern Cookery* (Heinemann)

Fuller, *Modern Restaurant Service* (Hutchinson)

Fuller and Currie, *The Waiter* (Hutchinson)

Fuller and Renold, *Chef's Compendium of Professional Recipes* (Constable and Heinemann)

Hering's *Directory of Classical and Modern Cookery* (Virtue)

HMSO, *Food Hygiene Regulations*

Kotas, *Accounting in the Hotel and Catering Industry* (International Textbook Company)

Kotas, *An Approach to Food Costing* (Hutchinson)

Kotas and Davies, *Food cost control* (International Textbook Company)

Kotschevar and Terrell, *Food Service Planning, Layout and Equipment* (Wiley)

Lawson, *Restaurant Planning* (Design Architectural Press)

Lawson, *Principles of Catering* (Design Architectural Press)

Morel, *The Caterer's Companion* (Pitman)

Raffael, *Bistro Style Cookery*

Reay, *Cooking for Large Numbers*

Riley, *Understanding Food Cost Control* (Edward Arnold)

Robins, *Food Science in Catering* (Heinemann)

Savoy Hotel, *Savoy Cocktail Book*

Schneider and Capisano, '*Can I Help You?*' *The French Menu Explained* (Edward Arnold)

Simon, *A Wine Primer* (Michael Joseph)

Smith, *Hotel and Restaurant Design* (Design Council)

Vandyke Price, *Directory of Wines and Spirits* (Northwood Books)

The HCIMA has a comprehensive mail order book service: c/o Eddington Hook, Vale Road, Tonbridge, Kent TN9 1XR; 0732 357755.

Business reading from Kogan Page

Consumer Law for the Small Business, Patricia Clayton
Financial Management for the Small Business, Colin Barrow
How to Buy a Business, Peter Farrell
Law for the Small Business, Patricia Clayton
Raising Finance: The Guardian Guide for the Small Business, Clive Woodcock
Running Your Own Catering Business, Ursula Garner and Judy Ridgway
Running Your Own Pub, Elven Money
Running Your Own Small Hotel, Joy Lennick
Running Your Own Wine Bar, Judy Ridgway
Taking up a Franchise, Godfrey Golzen and Colin Barrow
Working for Yourself: The Daily Telegraph Guide to Self-Employment, Godfrey Golzen.

Journals

Cash and Carry Caterer,
Thomas Reed Ltd, 36–37 Cock Lane, London EC1A 9BY
Caterer and Hotelkeeper,
IPC Consumer Industries Press Ltd, The Quadrant, Quadrant House, Sutton, Surrey SM2 5AS
Catering,
Dewberry Publication Services Ltd, 161–165 Greenwich High Road, London SE10 8JA
Catering and Hotel Management,
Link House Magazines (Croydon) Ltd, Link House, Dingwall Avenue, Croydon, Surrey CR9 2TA

Useful Addresses

Trade associations and official organisations

National telephone dialling codes are given, although local codes may differ.

Automobile Association
Fanum House, Basingstoke, Hampshire RG21 2EA; 0256 20123

Board of Customs and Excise and VAT Administration
King's Beam House, Mark Lane, London EC3R 7HE; 01-626 1515

British Franchise Association
Franchise Chambers, 75a Bell Street, Henley-on-Thames, Oxfordshire RG9 2BD; 0491 578049

British Hotels Restaurants and Caterers Association
40 Duke Street, London W1M 6HR; 01-499 6641

British Insurance Brokers Association
14 Bevis Marks, London EC3A 7NT; 01-623 9043

British Nutrition Foundation
15 Belgrave Square, London SW1X 8PS; 01-235 4904

Catering Equipment Manufacturers Association of Great Britain
14 Pall Mall, London SW1Y 5LZ; 01-930 0461

City and Guilds of London Institute
46 Britannia Street, London W1N 4AA; 01-278 4411

Cookery and Food Association
1 Victoria Parade, By 331 Sandycombe Road, Richmond, Surrey TW9 3NB; 01-948 3870

Craft Guild of Chefs
c/o Cookery and Food Association, 1 Victoria Parade, Richmond, Surrey TW9 3NB; 01-948 3870

English Country Cheese Council
National Dairy Centre, 5–7 John Prince's Street, London W1M OAP; 01-499 7822

English Tourist Board
4 Grosvenor Gardens, London SW1W ODU; 01-730 3400

Flour Advisory Bureau
21 Arlington Street, London SW1A 1RN; 01-493 2521

Food Hygiene Advisory Council
c/o Dept of Health & Social Security, Alexander Fleming House,
    Elephant and Castle, London SE1 6BY; 01-407 5522 Ext 6644

Fresh Fruit and Vegetable Information Bureau
9 Walton Street, London SW3 2SD; 01-589 6601

General Municipal, Boilermakers and Allied Trades Union
Thorne House, Ruxley Ridge, Claygate, Esher, Surrey
    KT10 0TL; Esher 62081

Highlands and Islands Development Board
Bridge House, Bank Street, Inverness IV1 1QR; 0463 34171

Hotel and Catering Industry Training Board
PO Box 18, Ramsey House, Central Square, Wembley,
    Middlesex HA9 7AP; 01-902 8865

Hotel and Catering Workers' Union
Thorne House, Ruxley Ridge, Claygate, Surrey KT10 OTL;
    0372 62081

Hotel Catering and Institutional Management Association
191 Trinity Road, London SW17 7HN; 01-672 4251

International Wine and Food Society
66–67 Wells Street, London W1P 3RB

Licensed Trade Education and Training Committee
The Brewers' Society, 42 Portman Square, London W1H OBB;
    01-486 4831

Meat and Livestock Commission
PO Box 44, Queensway House, Bletchley MK2 2EF; 0908 74941

National Association of Toastmasters
29 Kenmare Gardens, London N13 5DR; 01-807 4631

National Dairy Council
5–7 John Prince's Street, London W1M OAP; 01-499 7822

Northern Ireland Tourist Board
River House, 48 High Street, Belfast BT1 2DS; 0232 231221

Office of Wages Council
Steel House, 11 Tothill Street, London SW1H 9NF; 01-213
    3887. (Due to be closed, if proposed legislation is enacted.)

Pizza Association
4 Berkeley Square, Clifton, Bristol BS8 1HJ

The Restaurants Association of Great Britain
44 Old Church Street, London SW3 5BY; 01-589 7865

Royal Automobile Club
PO Box 100, RAC House, Lansdowne Road, Croydon CR9
  2JA; 01-686 2525

Royal Society of Health
13 Grosvenor Place, London SW1X 7EN; 01-235 9961

Scottish Tourist Board
23 Ravelstone Terrace, Edinburgh EH4 3EU; 031-332 2433

Small Firms Centres
All centres can be contacted by dialling 100 and asking for
  freefone Enterprise. There are offices in 11 cities.

UK Bartenders Guild
70 Brewer Street, London W1R 3PJ; 01-437 2113

Vegetarian Society of the UK
53 Marloes Road, London W8 6LA; 01-937 7739

Wages Inspectorate
London & South Eastern Region, Hanway House, Red Lion
  Square, London WC1R 4NH; 01-405 8454

Wales Tourist Board
Brunel House, 2 Fitzalan Road, Cardiff CF2 1UY; 0222 499909

Wine and Spirit Association
Five Kings House, 68 Upper Thames Street, London EC4V
  3BH; 01-248 5377

Equipment supplies

Advance Services plc
77–83 Upper Richmond Road, London SW15 2TD; 01-789
  6571. (Linen hire and cleaning)

Andy Thornton Architectural Antiques Ltd
Ainleys Industrial Estate, Elland, West Yorkshire HX5 9JP;
  0422 78125

G F E Bartlett & Son Ltd
Maylands Avenue, Hemel Hempstead, Hertfordshire HP2 7EN;
  0442 60222. (Kitchen)

Batchelors Cooking Supplies Ltd
Wadsey Bridge, Sheffield, South Yorkshire S6 1NG; 0742
349422. (Food)

Becas Soups
Blackhorse Road, Letchworth, Hertfordshire SG6 1HL; 04626
6971

Brake Bros (Frozen Foods) Ltd
Enterprise House, Godlington Road, Ashford, Kent

British Gas Corporation
326 High Holborn, London WC1V 7PT; 01-242 0789. (Kitchen
and consultancy)

British Textile Rental Association
Lancaster Gate House, 319 Pinner Road, Harrow, Middlesex
HA1 4HX; 01-863 9177

Cross Paperware Ltd
PO Box 3, Dunstable, Bedfordshire LU6 3HX; 0582 62361

Crypto Peerless Ltd
Bordesley Green Road, Bordesley Green, Birmingham B9 4UA;
021-773 1234. (Peelers, dishwashers)

Deeko plc
German Road, London N17 OUG; 01-808 5871. (Paperware)

Falcon Catering Equipment
Glynwed Consumer & Building Products Ltd; 28 Brook Street,
London W1Y 2PD; 01-499 8941. (Cooking)

Federated Potteries Company Ltd
Lambert Street, Tunstall, Stoke-on-Trent ST6 6AN; 0782
85621. (Tableware)

Foster Refrigerator (UK) Ltd
Oldmeadow Road, Kings Lynn, Norfolk PE30 4JU; 0553 61122

Garland Catering Equipment Ltd
Swallowfield Way, Hayes, Middlesex; 01-561 0433. (Kitchen)

General Foods Ltd
Catering Division, Banbury, Oxfordshire OX16 7QU; 0295 4433

The Hobart Manufacturing Company Ltd
Hobart House, 51 The Bourne, London N14 6RT; 01-882 6141.
(Kitchen)

Horwood Catering Equipment Ltd
Caterers House, 20 Selsdon Road, London E13 9BX; 01-472
1470. (Kitchen and consultancy)

ICL Ltd
85–91 Upper Richmond Road, London SW15 2TF; 01-788 7272. (Consultancy)

Jackson Catering Equipment Ltd
PO Box 153, Leeds LS1 1QR; 0532 702155. (Boilers and cooking)

Jacy of London Ltd
Brent House, Friern Park, London N12 9DA; 01-446 4211. (Clothing)

Leon Jaeggi & Sons Ltd
Helvetia House, 232 London Road, Staines, Middlesex; 0784 53967. (Utensils wholesalers)

The Kenco Coffee Company Ltd
Strathville Road, London SW18 4QY; 01-874 2272

Kent Dishwashers
Merrow Lane, Merrow, Guildford, Surrey GU4 7BN; 0483 373231

Lincat Ltd
Whisby Road, North Hykeham, Lincoln LN6 3QY; 0522 682911. (Kitchens)

Litton Microwave Cooking Products Ltd
Mint House, 6 Stanley Park Road, Wallington, Surrey; 01-773 1211

Max-Arc/Merrychef Ltd
Merrow Lane, Merrow, Guildford, Surrey GU4 7BN; 0483 37231. (Microwaves)

Melitta Catering Service
Humphrys Road, Woodside Estate, Dunstable, Bedfordshire LU5 4TP; 0582 600255. (Coffee)

Menu International
43 Northwood Street, Birmingham B3 1UL; 021-236 1427. (Menu covers)

Moffat Appliances Ltd
126 Morville Street, Birmingham B16 8DQ; 021-455 6544. (Kitchens)

Moorwood Vulcan Ltd
PO Box 16, Ecclesfield, Sheffield S30 3ZY; 0742 467121

NCR Ltd
206 Marylebone Road, London NW1 6LY; 01-388 8246. (Tills, accounting)

Oliver Toms Catering Equipment Ltd
222 Kensal Road, London W10 5BS; 01-969 8532

Oneida Old Hall Tableware
Bloxwich, Walsall, West Midlands WS3 3HH; 0992 401666

William Page & Co
Parke House, 130 Barlby Road, London W10 6BW; 01-960
2121. (Utensils, tableware wholesaler)

Primo Furniture Ltd
443–445 Holloway Road, London N7 6LW; 01-263 3131

W M Still & Sons Ltd
Fellows Road, Hastings, Sussex; 0424 432121. (Boilers, cafe sets)

Stott Benham Ltd
Vernon Works, Highbarn Street, Royton, Oldham OL2 6RP;
061-624 9681. (Kitchens)

Sweda International
Litton House, 27 Goswell Road, London EC1M 7AL; 01-253
3090. (Tills, accounting)

Valentine Equipment Ltd
4 Trafford Road, Reading, Berkshire RG1 8JS; 0734
51344/507722. (Fryers, hot cupboards)

Wedgwood Hotelware
34 Wigmore Street, London W1H OHU; 01-486 5181.
(Tableware)

Zanussi CLV System Ltd
310 Western Road, London SW19 2QA; 01-640 3477. (Kitchen)

Consultants

Gilstock Ltd
48 Market Place, Brackley, Northamphire; 0280 702641

Greene Belfield-Smith & Co
20 Kingsway, London WC2B 6LH; 01-405 3861

Melvyn Green and International Associates
18 Wood Street, Kingston-upon-Thames, Surrey KT1 1UD;
01-549 9557

Horwath and Horwath (UK) Ltd
84 Baker Street, London W1M 1DL; 01-486 5191

Society of Catering and Hotel Management Consultants
PO Box 28, Richmond, Surrey TW9 1BX; 01-940 6080

Estate agents

Robert Barry & Co
39 Upper Brook Street, London W1Y 1PE; 01-491 3026
Christie & Co
32 Baker Street, London W1M 2BU; 01-486 4231
Sidney Phillips
Eaton Bishop, Hereford HR2 9UA; 0981 250333

Index